Computers and People explains in lucid
and practical terms what machines can and
what they cannot do. It discusses the
economics of computers, describes in lay
terminology the basic equipment, and
explains how and why computer systems
require compromises and changes in existing
office techniques. The social problems
created by mechanization are dealt with, and
the author concludes with a realistic
preview of new applications for computers.

John A. Postley is Executive Vice President
and a Director of Advanced Information
Systems, Inc. He has previously worked for
The RAND Corporation as Head of the Data
Processing Group of the Logistics Depart-
ment, as well as Hughes Aircraft Company,
the Northrop Corporation, and at UCLA.
Mr. Postley is International Chairman of the
Special Interest Group on Business Data
Processing of the Association for Computing
Machinery, and a member of the American
Society for Public Administration.

"I've had it explained to me, but I still don't understand it."

Computers and People

John A. Postley

McGraw-Hill Book Company, Inc.
New York   Toronto   London

COMPUTERS AND PEOPLE

First McGraw-Hill Paperback Edition, 1963

To Judy

Preface

ALMOST FROM THEIR inception, over a dozen years ago, it was expected that electronic computing machines would eventually be applied to problems of business and to other everyday events. Now that the first steps have been taken actually to use them in this way, we have found these applications much more complex than at first they seemed. It is toward an understanding of these applications and their complications—and toward an understanding of the role of computers in dealing with them—that this book is dedicated.

By making extremely rapid arithmetic and logical manipulations possible, computers have already permitted us to carry out extensive arithmetic operations totally impossible without them. Now, as we begin to move into the sphere of business, it is becoming evident that entirely new methods of business operations and management are also possible by similar means. But while new triumphs in arithmetic could be derived from a sound basis of mathematical theory and research, no such basis exists in the business field.

It has been my experience that this fact is not well known. People like computers because they are modern, or mysterious, or prodigious, or because they think they save money (which they rarely do); people are rarely interested in computers because they know that the machines will open the door to the entirely new techniques of business operation and control which are so vitally needed in our increasingly complex business society.

My objective in this book has been to assess the impact of the digital computer and its related components on the day-to-day activities of ordinary people—especially those in business—as well as on those people more closely associated with the computers themselves. Therefore, this book should be useful as the basis of a general survey course for the college student whose specialization does not specifically involve the use of computers. It should also provide a much needed and often lacking understanding of the environment in which a computer must be used to those who are being trained to design and use it. And finally, it is my hope that the layman with a curiosity about the subject will find this book interesting and informative. All these people will find that this is not a "how to" book; it attempts to look behind the *how* at the *why* which dictates it.

I am indebted to all those unknown and unmentioned persons in the field whose ideas have formed the basis for much of what I have written; whenever the source of my information was known to me, I have cited it directly. I must express my special thanks to Dr. Robert M. Hayes, of the Magnavox Research Laboratories in Los Angeles, who read my manuscript and made numerous valuable suggestions. In most respects, I think the information presented here is accurate, but wherever it is not, the responsibility is entirely mine. In such a fast-moving field as this, it is probably not possible to publish a book whose contents are entirely up to date.

John A. Postley

Contents

Preface vii

1. The Relationship of Electronic Computers to Business Activities 1

Computer Objectives
Complex Operations
Electronic Computers and Large Volumes of Data
The Cost of Data Processing
A Look at the Future

2. The Tools at Hand 23

Early Computing Devices
The Functions of Modern Equipment
Data Processing Systems

3. Fitting Equipment to the Job 44

Introduction
Selection of Strategy
General Equipment Considerations
Procedural Flexibility
Electrical Communications in Computer Systems

4. New Concepts of Operation 63

Elements of Data Processing Activity
Accumulation of Basic Information
Generation of Operational Data
Processing of Data

ix

Result Presentation and System Response
Cost as a Basis for Comparison
Anomalies of an EDP System
Long- and Short-range Planning

5. Decision Making   **94**

A Definition of Decision Making
Elements of Decision Making
Complex Information Processing as a Tool in Decision Making
Data for Decisions
Humanism in Decision Making

6. Hardware Horizons   **120**

Engineering Developments
Future Equipment Concepts
Design and Construction of Computer Systems of the Future
Beyond the Horizon

7. The Role of the Manufacturer   **149**

Objectives and the Computer Manufacturer
Research and Development
Sales and Applications
Equipment Operation
Equipment Maintenance

8. Problems of Transition   **173**

The Computer Antagonizes Existing Procedures
Effects of Transition on the Individual
The Transition of Our Business Society

9. The Present Bespeaks the Future   **197**

The Climate for Growth
The Application of Digital Computers to Current Problems
New Vistas for Computers
Machine Abstracting and the Translation of Languages

Index   **243**

CHAPTER 1

The Relationship of Electronic Computers to Business Activities

ACTIVITIES CARRIED OUT by people in a business organization can be classified basically into two kinds: the activity of policy making and the action necessary to carry out the policy.

Policy making describes the job of deciding what *should* be done. It is carried out by people acting as "managers," and usually implies some action by devices or by people other than the policy makers themselves. The basis for choosing a particular policy is sometimes analytical, sometimes intuitive, and often experimental. Often the policy selected is chosen for no other reason than that it is the most obvious or convenient one to select at the time the decision is made. Even the time at which a particular policy must be adopted is the result of a policy decision similar in form to all other policy decisions.

The function of the action people is to *carry out procedures* designed to implement the policies given them. Businesses are intended to be organized so as to provide a maximum opportunity for this vital management-operating relationship. As a practical matter, however, it is extraordinary if, despite the organization for the purpose, action people are able to execute these management policies without error or question. That is, the action group tends to misunderstand, purposely alter, or be unable to implement the policy set forth by the policy group. To the extent that they carry out a policy other than the one specified by the policy group, the action group acts as a policy group, and some of the policy function is shifted to them.

Typically, the approach to the problem of data manipulation toward some end assumes that there exists some omnipotent body of people which can specify, without ambiguity and with all essential detail, the characteristics of the problem and the rules for reaching any of the possible alternative solutions. Yet experience reveals that such omnipotence does not exist. This fact, together with the fact that business operations must depend upon some basic policy, suggests that this basic policy is alternately that of the policy group and, where management policy proves inadequate, that of the action group.

With the recent arrival of the large-scale digital computer on the scene, the assertion can be made that the means are now at hand to eliminate the need for omnipotent management and omniscient operators and thus obtain the solutions specified by the policy group. Today's computer operates in a completely rigorous fashion. The trend is such that these marvelous machines will have automatic accessibility to greater and still greater amounts of information. Such machines will have the capability to take account of more and more contingencies and ramifications with respect to this information in order to achieve continually better solutions based on the available facts. Thus, theoretically, computers can carry out management's data processing policy precisely. Yet it will be necessary to improve substantially the data processing systems which utilize these machines in order to use this ever-increasing capability in an effective fashion.

It is to this gulf between these theoretical capabilities and the portion of these capabilities which we are actually able to realize that this book will be addressed. The advantages of the full employment of these theoretical capabilities are so great as to establish the goal of their attainment as essential to our continuing progress. As important decisions in our society grow more complex, the need to bring more facts to bear on them increases. Since problems can be formulated in which human competence to make decisions has been exceeded, automatic decision making becomes essential. In Chapter 5 we discuss the process of complex decision making with digital computers in some detail.

In a rather superficial way, many people are taken with the glamour of automatic handling of data and so in some sense believe stories they hear about the fantastic potentialities of computing machines. Indeed, we shall try to show that these stories are difficult to overstate. The term "electronic brain"—as it has come to be used to describe large-scale computing machines—suggests the awe and admiration in which they are popularly held. But we must distinguish between the actual *fact* that computing machines can realize certain potentialities, and the failure of *acceptance* by management or operating people of the computer as a tool to perform, in a particular environment, functions well within these potentialities.

Another perhaps more subtle area of misconception is contained in the supposition that the *essence* of computer capabilities is the ability to achieve results more speedily and accurately. The misconception is the assumption that speed and accuracy *usually* represent a major portion of the potential profit from a computer system. There are in reality examples which tend to support this assumption. The production of a payroll or the inversion of a matrix may require only increased speed and accuracy for improved results.

But it is in the ability to bring to bear additional and pertinent facts, either directly or according to some limiting criteria, that the most important potentialities of large computing machinery will eventually be realized. While clerical operations represent most of the existing computer successes, complex decision making holds far greater promise for the future. Predicting the outcome of elections or football games by analysis of current data and comparison with a mass of historical data to spot trends are already familiar popular examples of successful applications of this potentiality. Sales and inventory predictions by similar techniques are examples of profit-oriented applications which have also met with some success. To increase the incidence of this fundamental advantage, the question, "What, more than an increase in speed and accuracy, does this computer application represent?" should be posed with respect to every computer application.

The term "data processing" has achieved a remarkable degree of ambiguity during its relatively short existence. Some of the things which the term is used to describe include the *engineering* of devices which automatically collect and record information generated by some physical device such as a wind tunnel, the use of a control device such as a digital computer to *process* this information, the communication and computation *system* of which this control device is a part, the *mathematical* techniques by which such operational data are handled, and the development of *procedures* (which may utilize a computer) for the realization of the functional objectives of a business concern. It is this last definition of data processing which will be employed in this volume, perhaps to the consternation of people in other fields, but with good reason. In declining the other definitions, we further imply that the profession of digital computer programming is on one fringe of data processing, and that the activities of systems analysis, operations analysis, and operations research (as they apply to data processing) are at or beyond the other fringe. This focus of data processing on the interrelationship of computers and business may indeed be a crucial one as we are faced increasingly with digital computers in the business culture of today.

Data processing can be said to consist of three phases: the introduction of data into the system; processing, storing, and communicating information; and the presentation of results. Phase one comprises the collection of the information (data) necessary to reflect the policy set forth and the events which have taken place, and of the preparation of these data in a form suitable for processing. Phase two comprises the manipulation of those data according to logical or mathematical rules provided exogenously so that this analysis of them can be made, storing data for use in this processing and for use elsewhere in the system, and communicating among the three phases. Phase three comprises the presentation of outputs resulting from the processing phase to the appropriate persons for their information and/or action.

By considering the data processing activities of an organization as simply another functional element of that organization, along with such things as manufacturing, sales, inventory control, and financial accounting, we see that there are certain fundamental ways in which the operation of the organization can be improved by improving the data processing.

The first of these is to achieve "better" data processing in terms of increased accuracy and in terms of the capability for increased complexity. If activities carried out by people are replaced by activities carried out by machines, a significant improvement in accuracy can usually be achieved. Thus we strive to have as much of the input data as possible entered into the data processing system and manipulated to produce the desired reports or actions automatically by the machine. The requirement for increased complexity stems from the necessity to consider more data pertinent to the decisions made. Often the simple decisions of the precomputer system—based on judgment (guesses)—are replaced in the computer system by complex decisions involving many kinds of data related by a formula which expresses the policy to be carried out.

Faster entry and processing of data, per se, is the second way in which the data processing function may improve the operation of the firm as a whole. It may be the case, in a particular situation, that the value of the results contained in reports diminishes rapidly with age. Reports that sales in a certain section of the country are falling off are useful in helping to alleviate the situation if they are available in time but are of only secondary interest if they are known several months later. Whenever system response must await the processing of the data and this delay is costly in some sense to the efficiency of the system as a whole, the need for faster processing is apparent. This is the case when the repair of a vehicle must await the processing of data pertaining to the spare parts necessary for that repair.

It is important to distinguish between the need for faster processing, item by item, and the need for a faster processing rate albeit a longer time per item. These are often conflicting needs and must be considered as alternatives in each example encountered. We shall discuss this conflict and some of its implications in Chapter 3.

One of the most popular advantages advertised on behalf of electronic data processing equipment is that of direct dollar savings. However, while such savings can probably be achieved in some cases (even though very few such examples can be cited today), the most important data processing dividends are not normally to be found in this area. Net savings provided by such things as personnel and floor-space reductions offset by increases in equipment and unit personnel costs are not likely to be a major consideration. It is the indirect cost savings due to the better and faster data processing mentioned previously which are destined to be the champion of advanced data processing hardware and techniques.

Finally, one particular saving expected of electronic data

processing hardware and techniques may prove to be the most crucial of all. [This is the potential saving of manpower to accomplish the data processing job. True to a certain extent in industry, it is much more true within the government environment that it may become more and more difficult, and finally impossible, to obtain a sufficient number of people to accomplish the data processing job which we deem necessary. Even though the people required to develop and use data processing systems employing electronic hardware require more training and hence cost more than those required to operate manual systems, a (small) dollar saving may be realized after the change-over. A much larger saving, purely in terms of numbers of people, can usually be expected in large systems. In some situations it is this manpower saving which is the major one dictating the use of electronic data processing equipment, especially in situations where the work load increases or the personnel force must be cut or both.

While the existence of a potential manpower saving due to a new system may be real and significant, sometimes it is not achieved. The tendency, when an excess of manpower does develop, to try to do more with the personnel and equipment available, rather than to reduce the available resources to the new lower level required, is usually the culprit. Some of the many reasons for this will be discussed in Chapter 8.

Some examples of cases where these improvements in data processing have already been achieved will illustrate our point. Although not all these examples can be duplicated—or are appropriate—in every case, these kinds of benefits represent a key to our continued economic advance.

The accurate processing of large amounts of data according to complex criteria is the basis for scientific management techniques now being developed and tested. The scheduling of production is a case in point. The interactions among events which take place on the production line of a major product are so varied as to defy their complete specification to date. But with their identification appearing imminent, the use of a digital computer to process the data within the numerical relationships defined promises to provide us with a logical unemotional resolution of production-line problems.

Data processing speed alone can be a major advantage. Railroads have found, for example, that the rapid processing of their bills of lading has enabled them to collect much more quickly appropriate cross charges for shipping. Since an average of twelve cross charges are involved in each rail shipment, quicker billing and collecting which generates better utilization of cash reserves can mean the difference between an operating profit and a loss.

Economy per unit of work, formerly thought to be the main advantage of modern data processing techniques, has sometimes been found to be of secondary significance. Yet in the "bread and butter" application of payroll preparation, the reduced cost of accomplishing a large volume of work has often provided the wedge by which the data processing equipment could be procured for bigger and better purposes.

As our society's requirements to process data increase without apparent limit, it is in providing the resources to carry out this processing that the digital computer seeks its greatest advantage. Recognizing long ago that, with the present rate of business expansion, not even the entire fe-male population of this country would be adequate to han-dle manually the telephone traffic of the future, the tele-phone companies foresaw the essentiality of automating their toll-call business. The present trend in the data process-ing field seems clearly to reflect a similar pattern for the future.

Computer objectives

The objectives for utilizing large-scale computers in a particular business firm must be reformulated in terms of the future. Present objectives, formulated by accepting the constraints of past or present capabilities in data processing, are not likely to be suitable. Yet this reformulation is rarely carried out.

Computers and their associated peripheral hardware can be introduced into data processing systems in order to achieve one or more of three kinds of objectives. These objectives do indeed overlap, but are sufficiently distinct to discuss separately. They are (1) to deal with increased com-plexity in data processing, (2) to deal with increased vol-umes in data processing, and (3) to reduce data processing costs for a given level of complexity and volume. All these objectives usually involve increased timeliness and accuracy requirements.

The digital computer does not, *in itself,* provide any-thing beneficial. This is the first and most important fact to realize. What it does provide is the *capability* to implement desirable complex and voluminous data processing operations not achievable by manual or punched card methods. Computers do not integrate systems functions, although they often provide the *means* to integrate operations when integration is a desirable objective. The use of large-scale computers need not bear at all on the decision as to which management system should be employed, although it may make *feasible* either centralized system management or dispersed system management. And in any management system, the proper use of digital computers as a tool can *allow* that system which may be required to achieve the system objectives to function at the greater level of complexity and volume.

The underlying idea here is that the system objectives are developed for the purpose of improving management. To the extent that they approach the ideal management system, such objectives may involve new paths of data flow and new processing procedures. When the complexity and volume requirements defined by these objectives so dictate, digital computers and associated equipment can be introduced as a means to extend the limits of data processing capability far beyond those which may be realized without them. Although this suggests that the system objectives must be established first and that a computer is then introduced as a means to achieve these objectives, the original objectives cannot be considered fixed. Often they must be reduced, redirected, or otherwise altered to enable their achievement in the practical situation by whatever means (computer or manual) is actually available.

To be unable to identify specific problem areas in terms of volume, complexity, cost, and the particular ways in which each will benefit from the use of a large-scale computer is to lack a comprehensive plan for introducing an electronic computer in support of day-to-day operations of a particular commercial firm.

Complex operations

As business operations become more complex, the data processing systems designed to support them also tend to increase in complexity. This data processing complexity is of two kinds: (1) that of the individual operations involved and (2) that of the interactions among the many individual operations, simple or complex.

Consider some examples of complex individual operations. Where the act of requisitioning an item from inventory formerly represented a relatively simple isolated operation involving as explicit information little more than the stock number and quantity of the item required and the authority for ordering it, modern systems of inventory control imply such additional information as stock number of the next higher assembly, serial number of the item, the condition of the item returned, weight, cube, essentiality of the item, and the number of operational hours on the item replaced. Successful operation of these modern systems does not allow an option with respect to inclusion of the pertinent information of this type. Inclusion of this information is mandatory; to the extent to which data is omitted or erroneous, the system fails.

The well-established unreliability of people, as regards complete and accurate data input, immediately suggests that automatic input of much of the pertinent information is an essential requirement to extend this completeness and accuracy beyond the relatively narrow limits of people and into the range required by the mechanized system. A system whose basis is raw input data, and which does not benefit from repeated reanalysis of these data by people, simply cannot operate with incomplete or inaccurate data.

Modern systems for the replenishment of inventory depleted by requisitioning action provide another example of increased complexity. They typically involve numerical operations to compute "optimum" reorder points and reorder quantities which are relatively complex as compared with the systems with which we formerly dealt. Such computations are likely to be beyond the capabilities of the people who would be required to carry them out, that is, the people now operating the manual system. Here again the need for a digital computer system as a means to accomplish a series of complex operations is apparent.

In a sense, the whole purpose of many modern data processing systems is to provide a framework for decision making which is as closely related to all the pertinent facts as possible. This fact suggests the second kind of complexity —that of functional interactions. A computer system can usually be used more advantageously than just to produce larger and more frequent management reports. In fact, in so far as management reports serve to provide diverse information to people for decision making which involves a straightforward application of established rules to this information, the computer system should be employed as a means for making the decisions. Under such operation, the information involved in the reports is used by the computer for this purpose, and the explicit production of the reports as such is often eliminated.

The planner must take seriously the popular admonition to rethink the entire system in the light of new and vastly improved capabilities. For example, while normally one must employ expensive extraordinary procedures to expedite priority requisitions because routine procedures are too slow, a substantial improvement in the routine procedures may make extraordinary procedures for priorities unnecessary. Thus the system objectives may be to improve routine procedures sufficiently to permit the complete elimination of special procedures for priorities.

All this suggests that the data processing puzzle is composed of thousands of pieces, each of which must be used only in the proper place. Failure to do so results in decision making based on incomplete data, while the insertion of extraneous pieces of the puzzle where they are not actually required may be confusing, time-consuming, and costly.

When the details of these operations can be specified once for all, data processing systems employing large-scale computers can provide the means to implement systems vastly more complex than human capabilities will allow as a practical matter. Here again, the systems are not complex as a result of employing the computer, but rather systems involving complex operations and functional interactions become feasible as a result of this powerful tool.

Electronic computers and large volumes of data

A considerably more straightforward objective of developing systems employing digital computers is to deal with the problem of the apparently ever-increasing number of items, transactions, and operations occurring in many of today's business data processing activities. Although not all of today's operations involve more data processing volume than those of a few years ago, it is obvious that the general level of data processing volume is increasing rapidly because of population increase, increases in the level of our technology, and simply the passage of time.

A glance at some figures taken from the *Statistical Abstract of the United States,* 1957, provides a general idea of our national growth during the middle of the twentieth century. The population of the United States approximately doubled from 1900 to 1950 and is expected to be about 181 million in 1960. The gross national product (in constant dollars as of 1947) progressed from $149 billion in 1929 to a low of $104 billion in 1933 and then shot up to $330 billion in 1956. The number of civilian employees of the Federal government increased from 0.9 million in 1939 to 3.5 million in 1945 and settled down to a relatively stable 2.4 million in recent years. State and local government employees, however, exhibit a steady rise in number from 3.2 million in 1942 to 5.2 million in 1956.

Of more specific import to the field of data processing are the figures which reveal that total consumer credit rose from $4.5 billion in 1939 to $31.5 billion in 1957, that life insurance in force rose from 122 million policies totaling $106 billion in 1930 to 200 million policies totaling $372 billion in 1955, and that demand-deposit accounts in New York City banks alone rose from $327 billion and an annual turnover rate of 22.3 in 1944 to $815 billion and an annual turnover rate of 45.8 in 1956.

The rise in consumer credit suggests that the data processing problem of retail organizations in this one item alone has increased by a factor of 7 since 1939. The life insurance figures indicate an approximate doubling of the total data processing in this industry from 1930 to 1955. Perhaps the most striking are the statistics pertaining to New York City banks which imply that the data processing aspects of the banking problem increased in volume by about a factor of 5 in the 12 years from 1944 to 1956.

Success in coping with these gigantic increases in volume of activity may well depend on widespread introduction of digital computers into this business culture.

The cost of data processing

To begin this section it must be said that it is far from well established that any saving in direct costs can be achieved by replacing manual operations with computer operations in the commercial environment. There is presently every reason to suspect that failure to realize savings in computer systems over manual systems when problem complexity is concomitantly increased will continue to be the typical situation.

In many cases, however, it has been demonstrated that certain significant expansion in terms of volume of operations can be achieved with electronic data processing equipment at little or no *additional* cost, while a corresponding increase in the volume handled in a manual system would result in an almost corresponding increase in cost.

The point is that complexity is added in order to make systems better; systems are not better merely because they are more complex. Keeping this in mind, one can see that the added complexity of using computing devices often pays off handsomely; in fact, the conversion of this improvement into *in*direct but nonetheless very large savings is perhaps the major economy in data processing operations to be derived from digital computing systems. The high degree of complexity implied by many modern data processing concepts and systems and the very major savings resulting therefrom can often be achieved on a large scale only through the proper use of computers. Hence one may say that the savings accrued are due in large measure to the computer system which makes the new data processing system possible.

A look at the future

The nature of the future is that no one is in possession of facts concerning it. Available information concerning expected future developments may suggest that they are highly likely or very unlikely, but never that they are certain to occur or sure not to occur.

For this reason expectations about the future often prove to be wrong and are constantly changing to minimize this error. Hence plans made in view of these expectations must also change constantly. When these plans are insufficiently flexible to change as fast as the expectations governing them change (implicitly or explicitly), they are said to be in error. Finally we arrive at the interesting anomaly that, in this sense, the only thing in the data processing field that we can count on for certain is that our long-range expectations and plans will be wrong and will require change much of the time. Most of this book deals with data processing as it was and as it is. But in Chapter 9 we attempt to project into the future. In doing so, we realize fully that some of the ideas we express now will appear to be utter nonsense as we look back on them in the years ahead.

When the first large-scale digital computer was used in the United States in the period immediately preceding World War II, the event was received with a variety of attitudes. Qualitative predictions about the mathematical and clerical operations which these machines would accomplish were virtually unlimited. At the same time the corresponding quantitative estimates did not go far enough and in many cases have already been exceeded.

When the first computers began making ballistic calculations early in the war, some "experts" began to predict that soon all such "routine" calculations would be done by computers and that people would no longer be burdened with such mundane labor. In the early 1950s, when the digital computer was proposed as a commercial tool, equivalent optimism was evidenced as to the elimination of routine clerical operations. On the other hand, there were those who believed that the limit of the computer's abilities was represented by simple voluminous operations such as the ballistic calculations they were then doing and that problems arising in connection with data introduction into, and storage in, the computer system imposed very narrow limits on the work and machines could do. Statements to the effect that storage of 1,000 numbers within the system would satisfy all conceivable requirements can be found in the literature, although computers exist today which can store

64,000 numbers in the primary system and an essentially unlimited additional number in supplementary storage.

Today the potential computer applications in both the scientific and commercial worlds appear almost boundless. Indefinitely large amounts of information will be made automatically available to a processing unit capable of performing many basic operations (additions, subtractions, and simple decisions), each in one-millionth of a second.

Institutional and individual inertia, together with the substantial lack of knowledge about the many single operations which make up the complex business systems of today in the business world, are the major roadblocks which lie ahead. Although our knowledge about these operations and their interrelationships is increasing at a rapid rate, it seems likely that the art of applying digital computers to problems, and not the art of engineering the machines to do the jobs assigned to them, will (continue to) be the limiting factor in digital computer use.

The number of large-scale computers ($1 million or more) presently planned or in use in United States business, industry, and government is estimated at about five hundred. Medium- and small-scale machines ($50,000 or more) are presently planned or in use at an estimated level of three thousand complete systems. The dollar value of computer manufacturing replacement and service thus represented approaches $2 billion annually. The value of the activity made possible by their use, although impossible to estimate, far exceeds this figure. Estimates which appear reasonable place the total number of computers actually in use by 1965 at about fifteen thousand.

Although only about fifteen thousand people were engaged in professions directly concerned with the use (rather than the design and manufacture) of digital computer systems in 1958, this number is expected to increase to 160,000 by 1965. On the engineering side, over one hundred United States companies are now concerned directly with one or more aspects of the design and manufacture of digital computers, their components, and closely associated equipment.

What course can this development be expected to take from here? While it is undoubtedly true that many knowledgeable people expect this improvement and expansion in the computer industry to exhibit a tendency to level off, there is no historical reason for the pessimism. It has been reliably stated that in the period 1950 to 1953 more computing was done than the total of all computing previously done by mankind. It is likely that by 1957 this cycle was repeated. Moreover, it has proved to be generally true that the bigger and faster the computer is, the lower the unit cost for computing has become; i.e., the cost of a single addition or subtraction decreases as computers improve.

The term "computer generations" refers to those classes of computers such that each represents a completely redesigned system, incorporating all the latest engineering techniques over the previous one. Tracing of one family tree reveals an improvement of about a factor of 10 in the cost of a unit of computing for each of four generations introduced since the World War II era.

Rapid as development in the data processing field has been, there appears to be no reasonable sanction for predicting a decline in the development rate. New people and organizations are entering the field rapidly. Courses of instruction in data processing and the allied arts are hurriedly being added to the curriculums of American colleges and universities. There were less than five university computer installations at the beginning of 1956, about a dozen when 1957 began, and over sixty installed or planned at the start of 1958. Almost everyone in the accounting or production control departments of the country's large corporations has had some recent contact with digital computers operated by or planned for his firm. (In late 1957 one of the country's largest corporations was said to have a total of 60 computers, installed or on order, for various purposes.)

At the present time the United States appears to be well ahead of the other countries of the world in terms of volume of activity in the computer field. Nevertheless the field is advancing rapidly everywhere. In 1957, sixteen commercial computer installations were to be seen in Great Britain and fifty or more such installations were anticipated in 1958. Most of Western Europe—especially Germany, Sweden, France, and Italy—is becoming very active in the field, as is Japan in the Far East. Although little is known about computer activity behind the iron curtain, the U.S.S.R. is said to be about 2 years behind the United States in terms of technology, with most of the application confined to "scientific" rather than "commercial" (a somewhat ambiguous term when applied to the U.S.S.R.) problems.

Clever and resourceful as all this activity has been, it has not yet succeeded in making an important contribution to the job of identifying patterns of clerical and concept structure in terms of business data processing applications and computer characteristics. The effort required to select, define, and evaluate potential computer applications in a particular company remains much the same as it was a decade ago. The advent of a real "break-through" in this problem area, confidently to be expected within the next decade or two, foreshadows a far greater impact of digital computers on our culture than even our wildest thoughts suggest today.

CHAPTER 2

The Tools at Hand

BY MEANS OF THE mechanical components and electronic circuits of which they are composed, data processing machines perform such simple operations as the addition, subtraction, or multiplication of two numbers, or the transfer or storage of information. By combining thousands of these simple operations into a single second of automatic activity, these machines are able to execute highly complex mathematical and clerical operations very rapidly, and without direct human supervision.

The earliest examples of the modern data processing machine appeared shortly after the close of World War II. These devices were designed to perform these simple operations on only a very few numbers to produce an intermediate result. Thus they were able to compute the gross pay of an individual by transferring and storing the appropriate data and by performing the indicated multiplication of "hourly rate times the number of hours worked" in order to produce gross pay. The technique that was employed involved reading the set of data for each computation, executing a similar computation for each of the employees involved, and reading out each result, until the gross pay of each employee had been computed. The machine was performing identical operations on each of many sets of data, receiving data and producing results in a sequential fashion.

Present-day computers perform essentially the same simple operations of addition, subtraction, and multiplication of numbers. Additionally, they frequently compare the magnitude of two numbers or determine the alphabetic sequence of two groups of alphabetic information. Significantly, their capability to store information internally is much greater than that of their ancestors of a decade ago. By combining a great many of these operations on very large quantities of data, these present-day machines can solve, in a single complex step, problems of far greater complexity than the computation of gross pay. Such a problem might be the determination of the optimum quantity of a given item to produce in a particular manufacturing period, given the limitations of materials and manufacturing facilities and the cost and value of producing this and alternative items.

All the possible operations which might occur in the solution of such a problem must be completely specified to the computer. The technique for accomplishing this is called "programming." Only a portion of each "program" is actually executed in each complex step to which the program is applied. By directing the comparison of certain of the intermediate results computed with indicated criteria (externally supplied or also computed by the machine), the program selects suitable portions of itself and derives its results by executing these program "branches" as selective additions to the main program stream. Digital computers exhibiting this characteristic are called "stored program computers." The ability to progress step by step through any portion of the program which it stores, jumping from one part of the sequence to another according to the results computed on a particular step and thereby controlling the operations of the computer itself and all other components of the system, is the essential characteristic of a modern digital computer system.

The program is not actually a physical component of the computer system. Each of the simple operations of which the program is composed is retained within the computer as a set of coded electrical impulses corresponding to the component numerals, alphabetic characters, or special symbols of which the program may be composed. The program which controls the solution to a particular problem on a particular computer, however, is *in effect* a part of the computer. It must be specially prepared for this unique function. If either the problem or the computer is varied, the program must be rewritten accordingly.

Work is under way toward a universal programming system. By means of such a system, a program can be written to solve a given problem on any computer of adequate capacity. A few limited cases of this kind have been treated successfully very recently, but the lack of a general solution to this problem is probably due more to a lack of a precise definition of the problems to be solved than to any deficiency in the data processing technique. The distinction between performing the *stated* task and performing the *desired* task, easily made by humans, represents the last major barrier to all-out business data processing by a digital computer system.

Although the electronic computer appeared only after World War II, the evolution of the modern digital computer has been under way for more than a century. Since the advance to the electronic computer from manual data processing techniques is very great, let us review some of the major events which have taken us to our present state of development.

Early computing devices

The computing device which was the first to be developed is the abacus. Today this computing device remains the most widely used, although its use is confined mostly to the Orient and to the Middle East. It is commonly used there in even the most modern business establishments, and the clicking sound of the beads in use is common in a business office in Tokyo or Hong Kong. The abacus has been shown repeatedly to be equivalent to a modern electromechanical desk calculator in speed and flexibility, although its operation is considerably less automatic and therefore far more dependent upon the skill of the operator.

Among the earliest devices to perform such mathematical calculations as multiplication, division, and the extraction of square and cube roots were those invented by the Scotsman, John Napier (1550–1617). His were the first machines to perform the actual numerical operations without the participation of the human operator. Near the middle of the seventeenth century, Blaise Pascal of France developed a "calculator" with an ingenious mechanical arrangement. This device was probably the forerunner of the modern adding machines; indeed similar devices are marketed successfully today. Called a "home" or "pocket" adding machine, such a device is currently obtainable for only a few dollars.

Several other French developments followed that of Pascal. But about 1830, the Englishman, Charles Babbage, invented his "difference engine," the first successful mechanical computer design. Unfortunately, the required mechanical skills were not yet developed; so that, even with the financial support of the British government and the private fortune of Lady Lovelace, Babbage's efforts to construct a working model were unsuccessful.

In 1850, scarcely 100 years ago, the first keyboard adding machine—the Parmalee Calculator—was produced in this country. It added only a single digit at a time, and the maximum total was limited to 50. This device was followed by several similar devices. The Baldwin Calculator of 1875 marked the start of the American calculating machine industry. The year 1885 saw the Felt "Marconi Box," the forerunner of the modern comptometer. The Burroughs Listing Accountant of 1889 was the first successful machine to print its results and was the basis of the present Burroughs line. W. T. Odner produced a significant improvement in the quality of manufacture in Sweden in 1892, and thus founded that famous line.

In 1897, Dr. Herman Hollerith invented what was to be the forerunner of the modern punched card machines and the basis of the IBM line. His machines were first used by the U.S. Bureau of the Census in 1900. Electromechanically activated, the vertical punched card sorter was introduced in 1914 and was one of the first punched card machines produced.

These early computing devices now seem a far cry from modern electronic data processing systems. But they represent an essential stage in their development, just as the present machines will probably prove to be a crude step in the development of the machines of the future.

The functions of modern equipment

Equipment in a modern data processing system consists of several major kinds of devices. In addition to the computer itself, the system may include large-capacity facilities for storage of information, devices to enter information into the system, devices on which to record or display results determined by the system, and equipment for communication of information within the data processing system over either short or long distances. The required operation of a group of such devices under unified control and for a single purpose represents an engineering problem of a high order of complexity. In order to get a better idea of what is involved, let us consider the role of each of the elements of a computer system.

The Central Computer. The central computer, or "central processing unit," of a data processing system performs three basic functions: information processing, control of its own operations and those of the other elements of the system, and the storage of a limited amount of information required to accomplish this processing and control.

The processing function includes the execution of numerical operations such as addition, subtraction, multiplication, division; logical operations such as comparing information for equality or relative place in a given sequence; and the operations concerned with transferring information within and into and out of the central processing unit. Whatever their complexity may be, all calculations and groups of calculations can be described in terms of elementary operations of this kind.

The storage of processing and control data in the central processing unit has increased rapidly with the development of digital computer systems. Limited initially to only a few pieces of numerical information, it once was thought to have reached its useful limit at about 10,000 decimal digits of information. In a modern computer, however, the storage of a quarter million characters of information in this internal storage is not rare. Systems presently under construction will store internally 10 million characters of information, the equivalent of approximately twenty-five volumes of this book. Largely as a result of the increases in the speed at which information can be processed and the rate at which it is required for control, a continued increase can be expected in the internal storage requirements of a large digital computer system.

The basic components required to construct the *processing* and *control portions* of the central processing unit are essentially those of the ordinary electronic circuit. The critical difference is the very much higher quality components required in digital computer circuits over those required in the circuits of television or radio sets. Transistors, diodes, and even more recently developed electronic components are commonly used for this application. As in most other applications of electronic circuits, the once familiar vacuum tube is rapidly falling into disuse.

The basic elements of *internal storage,* however, have been developed especially for computer application. Originally employing relays and then vacuum tubes to "store" coded information, cathode-ray tubes (similar to those used as the picture tube in an ordinary television set) and magnetic cores (small doughnut-shaped objects about one-tenth of an inch across and capable of retaining a magnetic charge) were developed to form the internal information storage portion of computers.

In an effort to achieve the objectives of reliability, miniaturization, low cost, and high speed, the laboratory development of internal storage components continues. Taking advantage of the molecular structure of the storage material itself, the most promising development known today—called, variously, "molecular-level circuitry," "nuclear resonance," or "spin echo store"—is probably more than 20 years away. But according to present indications, we may in the future have a multiple storage component which will be completely reliable (subject only to the frailties of the devices which control it), store many millions of characters in a single cubic inch of space, cost only a small fraction of a cent per character stored, and provide information accessibility at a speed rivaling (and perhaps limited by) the speed of light.

Mass Information Storage. Serving a function rather different from the limited *internal* storage which is an integral part of the central computer, the storage capacity of a modern digital computer system *external* to the central computer may be very large indeed. Early computers, primarily for mathematical use, were not provided with any readily accessible external storage capacity.

External storage is employed primarily to record the "files" of the computer system in a form which is automatically accessible to the central computer. The time required automatically to make a particular piece of information, recorded in a particular external file, available to the computer—the "access" time—varies widely with the equipment used. Currently the range for automatic access to a single record is between as little as $\frac{1}{10}$ second (for a so-called "random access" file) to as much as 10 minutes (for some forms of magnetic tape). If the particular information required is not accessible automatically, the time of access to it may of course be much longer.

External storage for computer systems can in point of fact be described in terms of two parts: the storage *unit* itself, which "reads" or "writes" the information transmitted from or to other units in the system; and the storage *medium* from which the information is read or on which the information is written. Although the information storage medium is, in a few cases, an integral part of the storage unit, the more usual case is that these elements are logically and functionally separate.

Storage units are often very substantial devices, in terms of both size and cost. A single storage unit for reading separate storage media may represent as much as 10 per cent of the cost of the computer itself. Where the information storage medium is an integral part of the storage device, the cost of the combined unit may approximate that of the computer itself.

In either case, the storage unit is essentially a device which can recognize information coded on a particular storage medium and record coded information on another similar medium. The media for recording and reading this coded information may take such relatively familiar forms as punched cards, punched tape, or microfilm; or they may take the form of such specially developed media as magnetic tapes (relatives of the tapes used on home tape recorders), magnetic drums, magnetic disks (not unlike a large commercial automatic record player in appearance), or any of several other types of small discrete units on which information is recorded magnetically. Chemical storage devices are now under development and are likely to be employed widely in the future.

Storage *units* are relatively expensive devices compared to the storage *media* on which information is stored and from which information is read. As a consequence, one tends to restrict significantly the number of these units used in any one computer system. Wherever the information storage medium is an integral part of the storage unit itself, the total external information capacity of the entire system is therefore similarly limited. But where the medium for storage is separate from the device which reads or writes it, the information capacity of the medium is very large indeed.

Those devices in which the information storage medium is an integral part of the reading and recording unit are able in general to gain access to the information stored much more rapidly than are their separated counterparts. But since not all things are black or white, we find development projects in existence today which involve storage units with completely replaceable storage media whose access capability is very rapid indeed. These include devices to transport small cards with magnetic recording surfaces, and several other devices to store information on and retrieve information from small numerous storage media.

In terms of the practical limit to the amount of information which can be stored in a particular computer system, the factor of storage media replaceability is fundamental. With respect to space requirements and equipment manageability as well as cost considerations, the total storage available is severely limited in storage units where the storage medium is an integral part of the whole. Where the storage unit is separate from the storage medium, however, only a very few storage units are required to make the information recorded on highly compact storage media available to the system.

Consider, for example, the storage characteristics of a single reel of magnetic tape. Such a reel is approximately the size of a reel of professional motion-picture film. In this very small space, it can contain 10 million characters of information at a cost of less than 0.003 cent per character. Any number of such reels of tape can be read one at a time by a single storage unit, each in about 5 minutes. Thus the total amount of information made available to the system through the medium of magnetic tape is virtually unlimited.

Input. The information contained in the files, the coded program steps which set the pattern for the operation of a digital computer system, and the data reflecting events as they take place all undergo a process called "input" before their existence can be recognized by the system. Devices which accomplish this data-input function are integral parts of the system; these devices can enter coded information into that system, which information consists of numbers, characters of the alphabet, common symbols, or whatever else the coding is intended to signify.

Although it is possible for the occurrence of events automatically to trigger the input of relevant information into the computer system, an intervening manual operation is often required. Because such manual operations as the stroking of keys on a typewriter are inherently inaccurate, intensive research and development is under way to effect a reduction in the number and frequency of such intervening input operations. Direct input of information, automatically triggered by the event itself, can be found today where the computer system controls the flight of an aircraft or the progress of a production line. But in most data processing systems in business, the input of information results directly or indirectly from keyboard depressions by human operators.

Whether by automatic or semiautomatic humanly actuated means, information which is to be entered into the computer system is first recorded on a medium such as punched cards, punched tape, or the now familiar magnetic tape. This may be by means of actuating a keyboard, translating from one storage medium (e.g., punched cards) to another (e.g., magnetic tape), or as a by-product of another operation (e.g., the regular operation of a cash register). When the information has been recorded on the appropriate storage medium, it is made available to the processor as required by a suitable input unit. Thus data are almost never entered directly into a computer system by a keying operation.

Efforts to provide the means to enter information in its original form without further manual intervention are progressing rapidly. Gauges indicating such things as the reading of a compass, the wind direction, the position of a gyro, or the pressure in an oil pipeline are automatically "read" by newly developed devices. Techniques to read typewritten and even handwritten information have been successfully tested in laboratories across the country. Perhaps the ultimate in refinement will be achieved when research presently being carried out provides us with the means for input devices to interpret and code in computer language the utterances of the human voice.

In a strict sense, input constitutes the operation of communicating from people (or events) to the computer system. Similarly, output involves the reverse operation. Less strictly, however, the operation of entering information into the computer system from some intermediate storage medium (such as magnetic tape), on which it previously has been recorded by people, is referred to as input. Similarly, the intermediate storage of information (on magnetic tape) for the subsequent purpose of communicating it to people (or for initiating an event directly) rather than for retention in the computer system is referred to as output. Thus we do not distinguish strictly between the keying of information directly into a computer system and the keying of information onto an intermediate storage medium from which it is entered into the system. Nor do we distinguish strictly between causing a computer directly to control the operation of a printer and causing a computer to record information on an intermediate storage medium which is then used to control the operation of a printer. By avoiding this distinction, we hope to avoid a semantic problem now prevalent in computer circles.

The speed of input of information into a computer system is a highly variable factor and is sometimes dominant in determining the over-all speed of the system. Presently available input techniques involve a speed range of from the 10 characters per second rate of a manually operated keyboard to the 1 million characters per second rate of high-speed magnetic playback systems. Information recorded on punched card or punched tape media can be entered as rapidly as 2,200 characters per second, while readily available magnetic tape input systems operate near the 50,000 character per second range. By way of assessing the impact of substituting such speeds for manual operations, it is useful to realize that a champion typist is able to type at a rate of about 12 characters per second, so that the input rate of a single magnetic tape unit corresponds to the untiring simultaneous efforts of 4,000 champion typewriter operators.

Output. Just as it is necessary to enter from the world of reality all the information which is to be stored and processed by the digital computer system, so it is necessary for certain results of the processing, and for the contents of the files, to be reported to the outside world if they are to be of any use there. This process of extracting information from a digital computer system and reporting it to the people by whom it is required is known as "output."

Output can occur for many reasons. It might be for the purpose of producing the payroll check, of vital concern to each of the firm's employees. It might be concerned with informing an agent as to the status of airline seat availability, about which he had inquired, in an airline reservation system. It might be concerned with printing a schedule of events which should take place, according to computations made by the system, to achieve optimum results in a production-scheduling problem. Or it might be simply to inform the computer operator that the computer has finished the payroll and is ready for the next task.

But, unfortunately, in a great many applications the output which occurs is concerned primarily with reproducing for human perusal the contents of the files of the machine system. Although it occasionally serves a useful purpose, this kind of output is essentially a throwback to the systems employed before modern data processing equipment and techniques were available.

When a foreman needed to know the status of a particular item of inventory, it was useful for him to have on his desk a listing of *every* inventory item so that he could look up the *one* of particular interest. As a result of this requirement, the inventory records—where the inventory might have been of personnel (of spare parts, of money)—were listed daily and delivered to the interested supervisor (foreman, bank teller). Since modern data processing systems make possible the storage of this kind of information within the system and provide the means for ready access to it, it becomes no longer necessary to produce these frequent and voluminous reports whenever such modern systems are installed.

Today's outputs may be classified as those for action purposes, planning purposes, or in satisfaction of legal requirements. In due course, the fact that the processing of data and the maintenance of files can now be done largely within the data processing system itself will reduce substantially the number or size of the output requirements for planning and legal purposes and should increase the relevance of outputs for action.

Just as is the case with the input and storage of the system, the outputs can be described in terms of the media on which they are recorded. While not all these media can be read directly by human beings, they may constitute output in terms of their removal from the portion of the system which is automatically accessible to the processor, if their character is such that they can subsequently cause the operation of a device such as a printer whose output can be read directly by human beings.

Magnetic tape and punched cards are commonly used as output media, in much the same fashion as they are used for input. The use of punched tape for output is not unknown but is confined mostly to the smaller systems or to those systems which make use of punched tape long-distance transmission facilities. Magnetic tape output occurs at the same rate as magnetic tape input, in the neighborhood of 50,000 characters per second. Punched card and punched tape outputs occur much more slowly than their corresponding input rate, output being in the range of 60 to 350 characters per second. The large discrepancy between punched input and punched output speed is due to the fact that, in output, it is necessary to perforate holes in the punched card or punched tape stock, and the motion of the dies for this perforation is characteristically much slower than photo-electric or electrical input reading processes.

Because the output of a computer system is for the use of people, it can be carried out in a great many ways for a great many purposes—and in a few without any purpose at all. The stock-quotation boards now found in the offices of stock-exchange affiliates across the country are an example of an output of a data processing system, readily translatable to everyday facts. These large display panels contain several dials in association with each of the stock issues dealt with. Essentially the output of a data processing system, these dials reflect the most current price of the issue as well as some recent historical information about it.

The display of numerical results, textual information, or even graphs or charts on a television-like picture tube can currently be achieved as the output of a computer system. Such a display has the advantage of being able to show a great deal of information very rapidly and concisely and either to record it in this efficient form or merely to note it without incurring the expense of permanent recording when no file of the information is required.

An entire class of computer outputs can be characterized by the physical action which results directly from them. Such action might be exemplified by the movement of an aero-dynamic control surface in an aircraft or a hydrodynamic control surface on a ship. These movements result from the calculation of the geographical position of the vehicle with respect to its destination or some closer reference point, including such dynamic considerations as winds or ocean currents. A computer might also cause the opening or closing of a valve to control pressure in a pipeline at a chemical plant as a result of a calculation of the pressure in that pipeline according to some samplings taken.

Applications of this type have been called "digital control," although digital computers have not yet been widely used for these purposes. In almost every field where digital control applications have been developed, it seems likely that their use quickly to resolve the complex criteria involved and to effect the action resulting from this resolution is essential to the continued development of modern control systems.

Communications. The distance from a central computer at which either input or output may occur may be very small or very large indeed. If the input or output occurs from some place in the immediate vicinity of the computer, it is said to be part of the computer system. Until recently, however, if the input or output of the system took place at any great distance from the main computer, it was thought of not as a function of the computer system but rather as a function of a separate communication system. As the development of these "two" technologies proceeds, we are coming to realize that they are truly one. Thus the transmission of information to a digital computer for processing either from adjacent input equipment or from distant equipment located anywhere on earth—and not necessarily restricted to the earth's atmosphere in the near future—is now revealing its true significance as a computer system function.

This revelation has recently had several significant ramifications. In order to build a single unified system, communications and computer firms have found it advantageous to act as one in developing large integrated data processing systems for military use. Military networks initially identified as solely for communicating purposes have been found to require large computer systems to control the flow of data over the network, routing it to its ultimate destination of a computer center. Systems now in the development stages to assist in the airline reservation problem will connect several thousand reservation agents throughout the United States to a single computer containing the information they need. And the control of future space vehicles will be exercised, in part, over a radio communication link between the vehicle and a master computer system on the ground, thus welding the vehicle and its internal computer control unit and the associated ground computer system into a single operating unit. The present problems of determining the exact format of such vast and complex systems far exceed the technological problems of achieving this end.

Data processing systems

Data processing systems come in many sizes and shapes and contain the kinds of equipment described above in widely varying degrees of completeness. As computer systems grow more complex and more expensive, they are likely to be increasingly different from each other. It can probably be said that, lacking some positive effort to the contrary, no two large-scale systems now in operation have exactly the same equipment complement.

The use of the terms "large-scale," "medium-scale," and "small-scale" is widespread in computer circles. Despite this fact, it is poorly defined. For one thing, the notion of what is really large, for example, tends to shift upward as time goes on, to the extent that computers which once were considered large-scale are now usually referred to as medium-scale computers. This is not unreasonable if we think of the words as applying to size and computing capacity in terms of the present computer market, but it does tend to make the terms more difficult to define.

Perhaps one useful way to define these terms is with respect to the size of the capital investment they represent in the present market. Thus a large-scale computer system can be purchased for $800,000 or more, a medium-scale system for from $100,000 to $1 million, and a small-scale system for less than $200,000. In terms of rental costs, an "average" computer system in each class might rent for $30,000, $15,000, and $4,000 monthly, respectively, for each of the classes mentioned. Obviously unsatisfactory because they tend to generalize over a wide range of characteristics, these dollar categorizations are nevertheless useful as a rough guide to the value of the equipment involved.

The range of computer capability represented above is extremely large, even as compared with the price range cited. But even though this is true, it is not possible to make any quantitative statements about this range of capabilities without the detailed definition of a specific application in mind. Indeed, our ability to construct more and more powerful machines has grown so rapidly that a new "super" class of computer systems can now be referred to, priced in the neighborhood of $10 million and with a capability in some favorable examples as much as one hundred times greater than its so-called "large-scale" brothers.

Seemingly, as our ability to build still more powerful computer systems develops, the number and size of potential applications for them likewise increases. Whereas the first electronic computers were greeted with the statement that no more than ten of them would be required to solve all our problems, an estimated 250 large-scale computers, 1,000 medium-scale computers, and 5,000 small-scale computers are in current use in the United States. In view of the fact that a similar number of computers is presently on order for new or expanding applications, it seems clear that the scope as well as the number of applications of digital computer systems to scientific and business problems is increasing substantially. Corresponding to an investment of more than $1 billion, these computers on hand or on order represent a major new kind of manufactured product. When this figure is added to a like dollar amount expended for special military computers, it can be seen that the production of digital computers today affects, through both government and private business, the basic structure of our national economy.

CHAPTER 3

Fitting Equipment to the Job

Introduction

THE DEVELOPMENT OF a *present strategy* of business activity must precede the *design* of a large-scale electronic data processing (EDP) system intended to implement that strategy. It is nothing short of amazing how often this rather obvious principle is ignored. To develop this strategy we must strive to identify the *primary* purpose of the EDP system design and then to relate all secondary purposes to it in order of importance. Once a suitable strategy, which we will accept as fundamental at a given point in time, is thus established, the tactics by which these purposes are achieved by an EDP system can then *and only then* be described.

Let us illustrate the form of this strategy. It tells us whether our purpose is to add directly to the company's profits, reduce costs, or improve service to the customer; and whether these improvements are to be reflected as immediate reductions in company operating costs or primarily as "long-range" gains. Further, our strategy specifies the points in the organization at which decisions are made and the information required to make them. Only by clearly specifying these goals before the design of the detailed EDP system is undertaken can management maximize the probability that the resultant system accomplishes the purpose for which it was "intended." The fact that these intentions are likely to change over time must be reflected in the flexibility of the system design. This very imminence of change in intent dictates that system design must begin before the final detailed objectives are or can be known.

The choice of such goals, however, often depends upon EDP equipment considerations with which management is not familiar. It is also true that the people to whom these considerations are familiar are not likely to be the same people as those having a clear idea of the fundamental strategy of operating the business, mentioned above.

These facts suggest that the choice of a preferred strategy for an EDP system requires considerable study before a selection can be made. It is the purpose of this and the following chapter to outline some important considerations in this regard.

Selection of strategy

There are three areas in which thinking must take place regarding fitting data processing equipment to a particular set of jobs. These may be described as the areas where:

1. The objectives of the business organization clearly dominate the data processing considerations

2. There is the possibility of some kind of compromise between the apparent objectives of the business and the data processing techniques and equipment involved

3. The characteristics of the data processing equipments and techniques are unalterable at reasonable cost for the

portion of the problem involved and hence imply that the apparent object of the system must be changed to satisfy the data processing constraints.

The tendency is for business management people, lacking direct experience in data processing, to place too many of the subproblems into the first class. Thus management is likely to place excessive emphasis on the achievement of those management reports or those inquiry-response goals which appear today to be requirements of the system, rather than to attempt to reduce or remove these requirements for the new system.

Two examples will illustrate the point that apparently fixed objectives of company operation can indeed be altered by newly acquired data processing capabilities.

Consider, for example, the possibility that no daily or even weekly report of inventory transactions need be forwarded to the manager of a large inventory. In such a case, the persons responsible for the valuable inventory are apparently without the records of these items. But such a plan is realized by an inventory data processing system if a record of these transactions and the resultant inventory balance is maintained exclusively within the computer system. On the basis of these records the machine is programmed to reorder items for stock, initiate repair of reparable items, or carry out other "management" functions. Hence the machine is programmed actually to make some so-called "management decisions." By making management policy a part of the computer program, the real objective is achieved without the need to make the records themselves available to managers to read and study.

As a second example, consider the benefit to a large department store of knowing the status of a customer's charge account prior to any charge purchase by that customer. Whereas there are situations involving large dollar amounts which clearly require such prior information, other transactions, perhaps involving very small amounts, are advantageously completed prior to the execution of costly credit checks. Such a plan permits caution to be emphasized in the case of large purchases and customer relations to be emphasized in the case of small ones. This would place the capability to provide control over charge purchases in the class where some compromise must be made rather than in the class where the situation represents an absolute requirement to the system.

In reality much of the difficulty is concerned with deciding, in cases of conflict, the extent to which the stated objectives of the business or those of the data processing system designed to achieve the business objectives must be altered in the interests of the best over-all solution obtainable. The tendency is away from the middle ground toward one extreme or the other. Since a high degree of compromise is likely to be more economical than a purely management preferred system, and more operationally efficient than a system whose design is based entirely on hardware considerations, let us discuss ways in which these extreme positions can be placed into a perspective which allows the necessary compromises to be made.

The present chapter deals with ways in which job considerations affect and tend to alter the data processing system configuration. Chapter 4 discusses ways in which apparent job requirements may be altered by fundamental data processing considerations.

General equipment considerations

For the purpose of considering general types of equipment and broad system requirements, the function of equipment for processing data may be thought of as falling into two broad classes: that of performing specified logical and arithmetic operations on a relatively limited amount of directly accessible information, and that of making relatively large amounts of additional information available automatically (without human intervention) to these arithmetic and logical units. The hardware designed to perform these functions can, of course, vary widely as to speed of operation and information handling (i.e., storage) capacity. The basic task of fitting data processing equipment to a particular job or set of jobs consists, first, of defining the jobs in a logically acceptable way and, second, of improving the balance between the speed of the logical equipment and the size of the store.

Logical Operations. Although the range of primary logical operations which can be performed may vary widely among the so-called "general-purpose" computers of today, the ability to compound these operations provides that an essentially similar and very wide range of operations, e.g., add, subtract, multiply, divide, transfer information, and compare information, can be executed by any of these computers. The fact that the time required to execute a certain group of simple or compound operations to perform a particular logical job will differ greatly among the several computers thus constitutes the essential difference. To re-state: the distinction as regards logical ability of EDP equipment lies with the speed, not the range, of its logical ability.

Speed and Size of Computer. Deriving directly from this fact is the consequence that, if we hold all other computer characteristics constant, the requirement for speed in logical operations and size of internal (working) store tends to increase as the number of decisions assigned to the computer increases.

Consider, for example, an EDP system designed to execute reservation and ticketing services for a common carrier such as an airline or a railroad. Such a system may be limited to indicating only whether the desired accommodation is available locally or not. It may, however, proceed to investigate availability with respect to other legs of the trip known locally or remotely and even with respect to similar alternative accommodations. These alternative accommodations may either be scheduled or merely be designated feasible (e.g., a railroad may add an extra car on a particular train to satisfy a demand for travel at that particular time). Finally, the system may automatically produce the appropriate ticketing or it may simply indicate that a ticket can be or has been written and record the system reaction to this action. As suggested by this range of decisions that might be assigned, any increase in the number and complexity of these decisions can result in a corresponding increase in the requirement for computing speed and/or size of the internal store.

Another example exhibiting similar characteristics is the

now familiar one of payroll. The term "payroll," when used to describe an operation involving an EDP system, describes a minimum functional area to which the EDP system is applied. It is usually but not always the case that a great many other operations related to payroll calculations are or should be included in the application. The job of labor-cost distribution is frequently in this category. The questions of whether the payroll itself involves incentive and overtime pay, gross to net calculations, and different pay policies and periods are also pertinent. In one case a job requiring 2 machine-hours weekly was entitled "payroll," while in another case the "payroll" processing for a similar number of employees required 40 hours each week. In this example, the effect of increased job complexity under a given job title is reflected by the speed of execution by the system.

Size of External Store. Routine inspection of the data often serves as a valuable guide in the determination of the size of the external store necessary for a particular problem. The size desirable for this store varies directly with the amount of information to which the computer must have automatic access. Since the essential feature of an EDP system is to bring all the information pertinent to a particular (machine or human) decision to bear on that decision, the requirement for the external storage necessary to make this information available to the logical unit may be very large indeed.

To illustrate, let the reader consider a requisition for an item from a large inventory of say 100,000 different items. There typically may be two or three other items which can be substituted for the item requisitioned whenever that item is in short supply. Occasionally thirty or forty additional items may be substituted in certain limited circumstances. The set of substitutable items may be distributed physically throughout the inventory system. The total amount of information required in the worst case of such situations to describe the circumstances under which an issue can be made or another item substituted, and hence make a machine decision possible, is very large. In one example with which we are familiar, over 50,000 alphanumeric characters are required for every item of this type. A grand total of perhaps 200 million alphanumeric characters of information may be required to reflect the complete inventory situation in computer language, equivalent to something like 1 million sheets of paper or 2½ million fully punched cards for this particular example. Even today it is not difficult for the imagination to postulate requirements for files of over 1 billion characters, although we rarely run into such problems in practice.

Types of External Store. While selection of the *speed* and *size* of the logical unit and the *size* of the external store are relatively independent of each other and of all other features of the equipment, the *type* of external store which should be employed depends directly upon, and in turn affects, several other features of the equipment chosen. It is also true, of course, that the type of external store desired is related to the characteristics of the problems to be solved. One example of this fact is that, when the internal store has a high information capacity directly available to the logical unit, requirements for speed of access to various parts of the external store can often be reduced although its size requirement is not affected.

In the problem of inventory management discussed above, up-to-the-minute records, while of some fundamental importance, may not serve the ultimate objectives of the firm. For example, such records should not be established where their upkeep creates the excessive expense of decreased control and flexibility of the inventory management itself.

The ability to make a shipping decision for a particular item in a few seconds by omitting consideration of some of the pertinent criteria in order to gain this speed may be valuable when shipments must occur with equal frequency as, for example, in the dispatch of an item from a local warehouse to a fast-moving production line. On the other hand, the capability to make such a decision instantaneously is of highly questionable value when shipments occur only in large lots on a daily schedule, e.g., from a central warehouse in Middle Western United States to a regional warehouse on the Pacific Coast. In this problem, limitations of today's equipment are an important consideration, in that many devices available today which make possible these extremely rapid shipment decisions do not possess sufficient logical ability or internal memory capacity to consider many of the possible ramifications of any but the most straightforward decisions. It is confidently to be expected, however, that in the 1960s, data processing hardware will be available to overcome this difficulty.

Certain elements of contrast between the two major types of large external storage devices, sequential and random access, are crucial in the identification of the relative advantages and disadvantages of either as employed with a large-scale computer. The following paragraphs highlight some of the more important of these elements as they impinge on the objectives of the potential user of large-scale data processing equipment.

As suggested above, some idea of the size of file storage suggested by the term "large" is given by the range from 50 million to 200 million characters of information, although these numbers should not be thought of as lower and upper limits. Indeed, the definition of the word "large" depends to a large extent on the problem itself, having been known to range from 1 million characters to 10 billion characters or more.

The equipment comprising these stores can be classified as either sequential or random access equipment. Sequential access stores, typified by magnetic tapes, actually are sequential within each group (tape), totaling approximately 10 million characters each, but can be treated as random among groups; access time to items required in a sequence other than that of the file ranges from several minutes to several hours. Random access stores are typified by magnetic drums or disks; they are characterized by access times of from several milliseconds up to about 1 second.

It is important to note that two types of processing, not necessarily corresponding to these storage classifications, are involved. These may be called "on-line processing" and "batch processing." On-line processing involves the execution of an *entire group of appropriate operations* on each transaction that has entered the system before proceeding to the next *transaction*. Batch processing involves the execu-

tion of one or more (but not all) of the appropriate operations on the *entire batch of transactions* before proceeding
to the next *operation;* hence it involves at least two passes
of a transaction through the computer system. It is not
necessarily true that the need to "interrogate" the file dictates either random access equipment (since a form of random access may be possible with sequential access equipment) or on-line processing (since the problem may require
only access to information and not actual processing of that
information by the computer).

The main advantage of the on-line type of processing is
its ability to deal only with the file information relevant to
the transactions at hand, eliminating the need to deal in any
way with that file information irrelevant to these transactions. In some problems, this irrelevant information may
comprise about 98 per cent of the file for each cycle of
processing. The main advantage of batch processing is
that, for a given problem complexity, less logical capacity
of the central processing unit is necessary than in on-line
processing; this is due to the less complex job (discussed
previously) done in each pass on each transaction as compared with the random case. As the means become available, as we believe they will, sequentially to by-pass 98 per
cent of the information as rapidly as the remaining 2
per cent can be processed, the balance may tip in favor
of batch processing for a large class of problems.

Another important contrast is that of control, logical as
well as electronic. Control of random access devices is considerably more complex than that of sequential access de-

vices in terms of the computer program or the hardware or perhaps both. One of the primary reasons for this greater complexity in the case of random access storage is the need to place the identification key into one-to-one correspondence with the location of the item in the random access file when no mathematical relationship exists between the key and the location. This operation is often called "indexing."

Although the spectrum from sequential to random access is essentially continuous, the middle area is often particularly difficult to discuss without a specific application in mind. On the basis of the previous discussion, however, it appears useful to think of sequential access as a special case of random access (or vice versa) since access among sequential *groups* is truly random and these groups can, at least in theory, be made as small as necessary to reduce access within them to any desired time. Devices tending toward this characteristic are in fact presently available. By thinking of alternative devices (e.g., magnetic tape or magnetic disk file) in these terms, we may be in a position to answer questions relating to the preferred size of each access group and the optimum control configuration with respect to these groups for the specific data processing problems arising in a particular case.

Data processing applications today reveal a strong tendency on the part of the potential user to favor the "random access" approach over the "sequential access" approach. This tendency often neglects the distinction made above between random access equipment and on-line processing.

In particular it often attributes a far greater relative advantage to today's random access capability than it actually deserves while at the same time failing to take sufficient account of the incumbent *dis*advantages of today's random access equipment and processing. To state this thought in terms of the objectives of a commercial firm, it may be said that the true relative profit advantages of random access must be weighed against the corresponding costs incurred by failing to employ sequential access methods. As suggested in Chapter 6, research currently under way promises to provide us in the future with vastly improved random access stores. When these appear, the costs encountered may prove more favorable to random access storage.

The most obvious random access cost today is the direct one of more complex (i.e., expensive) equipment required to achieve it and the associated indexing for a file of a given (large) size. A typical cost of this type is presently about 1 to ½ cent per alphanumeric character stored in a random access device when the storage device selected is used at or near its storage capacity. The corresponding cost of a magnetic tape file is essentially limited to that of the necessary tape drive mechanisms and control unit, the cost of the magnetic tape itself being negligible with respect to the other equipment. The cost per character stored on magnetic tape ranges between 0.4 and 0.1 cent in the 50 million to 200 million character range.

An important related point is that such random access devices exist in fairly large units (e.g., 5 million to 75 million characters). For this reason, as the storage requirements grow even slightly larger than the capacity of the random access storage units on hand, a complete additional unit must be added at a correspondingly large increase in cost.

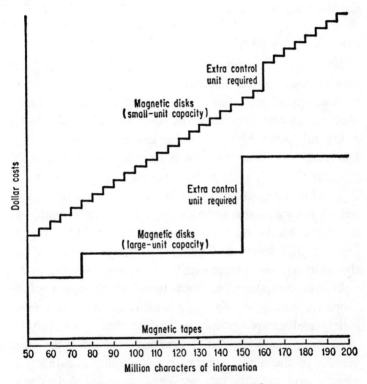

Cost Characteristics of Large Files

The figure illustrates these cost characteristics for three different kinds of large files: magnetic disk files of small (5 million character) unit capacity, magnetic disk files of large (75 million character) unit capacity, and magnetic tape files. Although the relative position of each curve with respect to the others may be altered by changing design or costing and manufacturing techniques, the shape of the curves is illustrative of the cost characteristics dictated by the three types of files.

Procedural flexibility

Selection of an over-all data processing strategy requires that the decision be made as to the degree of conformity with approved procedures and speed of response we *really* want our system to produce. In other words, are we always really in search of rigid conformity to procedures? The fact that this matter has been introduced for discussion suggests that in a great many cases the answer is "no."

The foremost reason for this is that in a significant number of situations the system designer is simply unable to anticipate all the events that will occur within the framework of his system, and hence the system cannot be designed to cope with these events when they do occur.

Digital computers, at least those which are working properly, cannot do anything which has not been completely and unambiguously defined to them previously by the data processing system designer. While one of the great benefits of the digital computer is its ability accurately to identify problem situations previously specified and to cope with them in a rigorous unfailing way, it also offers the corresponding ability to detect the occurrence of situations *not* previously specified in computer language and to bring these situations, as they occur, to the attention of management. The extent to which company operations can be completely described in order that they may be subsequently handled solely by the computer is a strategic decision of the utmost importance.[1]

The question of responsiveness—or speed of reaction—to changes in procedure directed by management is often equally as important as that of rigor. The difficulty stems from the fact that the system may actually be too responsive to such changes. In a production-control problem, for example, the system can be thrown into wild oscillation by the rapid introduction of "corrections" to the schedule. Such corrections, perhaps based on faulty data provided by panicky foremen or on transient circumstances which will correct themselves before any actual deficiencies are generated, can *cause* overages or shortages of parts produced for a particular end item far in excess of those produced in a system with slower reaction times. In such cases, if the action to correct the apparent shortages or overages is delayed, the response tends to be damped. Thus there are not only fewer corrective actions (less computing) required, but the slower response system may actually operate more effectively.

Electrical communications in computer systems

Systems design in data processing configurations involving geographically remote locations suggests that electrical communications be used between these locations. As soon as this fact becomes clear, the people to whom this idea is

[1] The suggestion is made later (in Chapters 5 and 9) that, to a large extent, computer systems of the distant future may be organized so that they can in fact handle problems which occur and have not previously been *specified* to them in detail, although a logical *structure* for defining must always be provided to the computer.

suggested feel that they are limited by the equipment available. That such is normally not the case is likely therefore to be a revelation to such people.

The facts seem to be that the task of fitting electrical communications equipment to the job is much more nearly possible at the present time than is popularly believed. Close proximity of the records to their potential points of generation and use is not usually necessary to effective data processing support.

The distribution of the information traffic which really must be transmitted, the distances involved, and the transmission speeds required are among the more important design parameters. As in most other data processing problems, the answer is not a single number for each question but an entire spectrum of numbers depending on a continuum of costs involved and benefits derived.

Networks or point-to-point transmissions? Leased wire or toll-call service? Voice telephone, punched card transmission, punched tape transmission, magnetic tape transmission, or regular United States mail? Considerations of these and other possible alternatives interact on each other in major ways and are in turn vitally affected by the objectives of the particular data processing system in which they are embedded. Here again the solution to the problem must begin with a statement of its objectives; only then can a satisfactory solution be assured.

The design of the communications portion of a data processing system is truly complex. However, a simple example may serve to illustrate some of its most important aspects. The table that follows illustrates the effect of some design alternatives under a particular set of assumptions, including:

1. Point-to-point transmissions
2. Five hundred mile separation between points
3. A message consists of 80 alphanumeric characters of information

No credit has been given for multiple use of toll-line facilities, such as can be employed by the IBM Transceiver. Neither has any system been charged with time or costs derived from the necessity for special advance preparation of the material for transmission, as required by the AT&T Dataphone system. And finally, the system considered in the 2,000 messages and the maximum rate case is not necessarily the same for a particular named system, e.g., toll or leased lines, punched or magnetic tape, etc.

Comparative Communication Ratios

Communication system	2,000 messages		Maximum transmission rate	
	Time-requirement ratio	Unit-cost ratio	Information-capacity ratio	Unit-cost ratio
Voice telephone ...	135	13	1	70
Teletype	22	2	6	10
IBM Transceiver ..	11	3	13	6
AT&T Dataphone .	1½	1	150	1⅓
Collins Kineplex ..	1	7	300	1

In spite of its lack of usefulness as a tool for designing communication systems, the table above does illustrate rather nicely a variation by a factor of 13 in cost for a relatively small requirement to send 2,000 messages. Far more striking, perhaps, is the variation by a factor of 70 in the costs among communications media when there is a requirement to transmit all the information the communications line will bear and hence to utilize the maximum information rate of such high-capacity systems as the Collins Kineplex and the AT&T Dataphone. Here, with a single set of terminal equipment (sending and receiving device at each end of the line), we have obtained a theoretical capability of several hundred thousand transmissions per day with this equipment.

The present discussion is intended to highlight some key points relating to present-day electrical communications capabilities and relative costs. In the most favorable case mentioned, the cost of providing electrical communications is almost identical to that of sending the equivalent amount of information on an appropriate number of fully punched cards by ordinary mail. Thus, surely, is rapid electrical communication of large amounts of information across complete systems entirely within the realm of feasibility and practicability now or in the very near future.

CHAPTER 4

New Concepts of Operation

RECOGNITION OF THE operation-management problems
which must be faced in the installation and operation of a
computer system in an existing business environment must
permeate the planning of the entire project. Only with a
clear realization of these problems is success likely to be
achieved.

Problem recognition involves an understanding of the
benefits which may be achieved as well. In most cases, the
objectives of installing and operating an EDP system in
place of manual or punched card procedures are likely to
be to extend those procedures so that they relate more
closely to the fundamental objectives of the business organization. Because this requires a precise definition of
these objectives, their complete reevaluation is indicated. In
these cases no longer do we try just to do a better job of
accomplishing the data processing procedures, but first we
restudy these procedures as part of the major objectives of
the organization and in terms of the new data processing
tools at hand.

Such an approach may involve a major upheaval in the
way people operate to perform their jobs. The statement

that "no psychological (including educational) and physiological problems *need* arise on the introduction of automation if the *proper* precautions are taken at all levels and in all parts of our social structure" was made recently by an expert in the automation field. Such a statement implies, perhaps, that it is not the essence of automation to perform processes fundamentally unlike those performed by people, and so it "need" not create related psychological and physiological problems. Notwithstanding the suggestion of science fiction to the contrary, it is entirely true that digital computers cannot carry out thought processes which cannot be duplicated by the people who build them or who operate them; thus there is no "need" for these psychological problems to arise if the "proper" precautions are taken.

We seem, however, to be faced with the rather embarrassing fact that, while "proper precautions" certainly do by their very definition eliminate the psychological problems introduced by automation, these problems do exist and are in fact what we believe to be the major barrier to the advance of automation in the culture of today. The very fact that at least a partial victory over the cultural problems arising out of the introduction of automatic procedures is possible implies, in the face of the very meager results achieved in this area to date, that the number of precautions which are indeed proper is almost infinitely larger than was at first thought and that the nature of these precautions is far from completely known at this time. Thus, rather than simply stating that the proper precautions will avoid the problem, let us examine these precautions in some detail.

Conveniently enough, the steps which must be undertaken to integrate a data processing system involving a digital computer into an existing business environment fall into two classes: those problems arising between the computer and the people who must generate its input or utilize its output; and those problems connected with integrating a computer into a business society consisting of people, as societies are apt to, rather than automatic devices. We shall leave the broader cultural discussion to a later chapter and discuss the relationship between data processing equipment functions and the functions of management in the pages immediately following.

One might begin the job of installing an electronic data processing system by specifying as clearly as possible the objectives behind the project. "Of course," you say. But we would estimate that in 75 per cent or more of the cases that have come to our attention in the business data processing field, the real objectives of installing an electronic data processing system were not clearly understood by top management, middle management, or the so-called "working level" people. Such possible objectives as a reduction in clerical costs, a speedup of report preparation, or the production of useful new reports not possible under the present system might very well turn out to be conflicting objectives. A positive understanding of the real objectives and the relationship among them may prove to be the key to early success in a new computer installation.

Elements of data processing activity

In general there are four parts comprising what might be called the "elements of data processing activity":

1. Accumulation of basic information

2. Generation of operational data
3. Processing of data
4. Result presentation and system response

Any decision as to whether large-scale data handling should be employed and, if so, which equipment, depends directly on considerations within these four elements.

Accumulation of basic information

In large-scale data processing problems, the jobs of accumulation of the basic information and its transcription into "machine language" are of major importance. In one inventory problem with which we are familiar, the job of accumulating in machine language the basic factual information on somewhat more than 6,000 different inventory items required a number of man-hours estimated variously at between 20,000 and 50,000, or at over 3 man-hours per item. This unenviable record was achieved even though that information was already in existence in punched card or manual form. Thoughtful selection of data-handling equipment with this function in mind and the utilization of advanced techniques for catalogue-data accumulation could have reduced this man-hour requirement substantially.

The magnitude of the initial data-accumulation effort required is often deceiving. Large files such as those of many insurance companies which have been accumulated over a great many years are likely to be so large as to require many tens of man-years simply to accomplish a straightforward "condensed" conversion into some language which can be read automatically by a machine. Ill-considered techniques of editing and checking this information may very well run the total time involved in initial file establishment for a large-scale electronic data processing system up to 100 man-years or more.

The need to consolidate existing files also appears to be a major problem in this area. A related problem is that of gathering new information not previously required and including it in the new file. A realization at the outset that the consolidated file is the object of this effort—and so the fewer intermediate steps the better—is likely to prove valuable. A useful gambit has proved to be to establish a single intermediate file, manual or mechanized, with a pigeonhole for each piece of information desired from the various existing files and upon completion of this file to re-record it in suitable machine language form if it is not already so recorded.

Devices now under development in engineering laboratories all over the country promise much in the way of relief from this major clerical job associated with conversion to EDP equipment. Microfilm readers and direct character-sensing devices are in the prototype stage in the United States, England, and Japan, although a great deal of work is yet to be done. The banking industry has been a major force behind the development of machines automatically to read and record information written in special magnetic ink or by an ordinary typewriter.

In order to avoid an overly pessimistic appearance we might mention a few favorable aspects to this problem. The most important such favorable aspect is that, however large the job of file conversion proves to be, it always remains a one-time job. Once the basic files are converted to machine language, the job need never be repeated. Further, although we must accept existing files in the form in which they presently exist, large files have a fortunate tendency to exist in punched card form. In the case of the Social Security Administration, for example, where one of the world's largest existing files was encountered upon conversion to EDP equipment, 120 million records were converted to magnetic tape by machine in the equivalent of only about a half year of single-shift machine operation.

Generation of operational data

Contrasting with information from which the basic files are formed, operational data are generated as a by-product of operation itself. These data are generated by each occurrence of the business operations they represent.

Collection and use of data generated are the pertinent problems. This involves considerations of necessity, convenience, and even feasibility of data collection and use in terms of the costs involved and the purposes served thereby. Events take place as a result of their environment; the question arises as to whether the benefits derived from collecting (and using) the data reflecting these events is greater than the economic and sociological costs incurred.

In those cases where one has decided this question in the affirmative, there are certain data processing hardware and techniques which can be employed to maximize the efficiency of the collection operation.

The essence of this maximizing process is the goal of getting the information into machine language after as few human transcriptions as possible are employed. A simple example of this is the completely automatic entry of the time, date, and location at which an item of inventory is issued to the ultimate user. Human beings are characterized, in part, by the fact that they tend to make a large number of errors. Whereas an electromechanical device to transmit alphabetic information presently makes about one error for every 40,000 characters transmitted, tests have shown that a qualified human operator will average one error in every 2,000 characters. Moreover, devices whose operation is based on electronic principles can now be expected to exhibit an incidence of error something like 100 times better than even the best mechanical device, and their record for accuracy is improving rapidly under increasing emphasis. Here too is an opportunity to "mechanize" an important data processing operation—data entry into the system—without creating psychological problems at the same time. Little question of ability—human or machine—arises here, although management reluctance to assume data-entry responsibility may remain a thorny problem.

Truly a key facet of a successful data processing operation is the correct entry of operating data into the data processing system. While this is true in any data processing system, manual or highly mechanized, it is far more significant in the latter case. The fact that the mechanized system is essentially rigorous while the manual system is capable of utilizing human judgment for corrective action implies that the effect of data errors in a highly mechanized system is much the larger. Thus the inclusion of procedures to ensure the accuracy of the operational data entering the system is beneficial to any system for processing those data and essential to a highly mechanized one.

Processing of data

The need to consider the processing abilities of the particular computing equipment under consideration as compared with the requirements of the problem is a relatively obvious one. The major consideration in connection with this element of data processing activity is that, just as the selection of the proper equipment to be used for a given set of commercial data processing functions is dependent on the functions themselves, so some of the functions done by the machine, or in some cases done at all, are dependent on the particular hardware chosen for the job. It is essential to remember that decisions which relate to hardware for a particular portion of the problem, failing to consider the problem as a whole, should be avoided. Thus, while one set of hardware may appear to provide a desirable solution to a particular requirement of a particular job (e.g., rapid handling of "priority" requisitions in an inventory-control job), it may very well produce such significantly non-optimum solutions to other important parts of the problem (e.g., the processing of the great mass of inventory-activity data against all the relevant parts of the master files) as to render its use for the problem inadvisable.

Dealing as it does with the operation of processing data as necessary for producing the results desired of the aggregate elements of data processing activity, the data processing element is the essence of the whole job. Consequently it will be dealt with in some detail in the next chapter on Decision Making.

Result presentation and system response

The fourth element of data processing activity poses the question: What information *should* be presented to management and to the system as a whole, and how should it be presented? We must therefore guard against answering the question: How can I best generate the data processing results of the system I have been employing in the *past?* It is easy to get people to agree to the distinction between these questions on a theoretical level, but it seems to be rather difficult to carry out the "preferred" approach in practice.

System analysis can show where changes are required. But where it appears obvious that certain reports should be altered or eliminated from the new, the inertia of the present system mitigates against change. And where new reports to serve now unserved functions suggest themselves, the difficulty of proving their value in advance often delays their start.

Daily *summaries* of the inventory position with only the troublesome areas reported in *detail* present an example of a new reporting function made possible by greatly increased data processing capacity. Such summaries eliminate the need for the production of an item-by-item inventory report on a frequent schedule, although they are likely to be based on a record of the item-by-item inventory position retained as a basis for further processing in the data processing hardware itself.

Again, as in the previous elements of data processing, the

main problem in implementing the theoretical design is essentially psychological. People are unaccustomed to accepting summary information from machines without receiving the detail information to support the summary. They are not "machine-oriented." Basic training in accounting is based on the fact that the detail must support the conclusions (as indeed it must). It is probable that only success, over an extended time period, of the electronic computer as an integral part of the data processing operation will build the confidence which we are suggesting. At the moment the level of this confidence in computers by potential "customers" seems to be well below the theoretical capability of the data processing art.

In a sense the quality of the result presentation and system response part of the data processing cycle represents the degree of realization of the objectives of the system. Since this quality depends in turn on the degree of acceptance of—and, to a certain extent, dependence on—machine results, the emergence of the true integration of man and machine in the data processing field must await the successful conclusion of the apprentice period by electronic data processing machines.

That this confidence is deserved and will come to pass seems certain. Already there are many applications in operation where customer resistance to the elimination or reduction of certain reports has been removed, not simply because of persuasive arguments on the part of the system designers but because these reports, presented as requested, actually proved to be excessively voluminous, detailed, and troublesome, and of little or no compensating usefulness.

For example, in one large inventory-control application where daily reports of inventory balances and transactions relating to them were thought (by the inventory managers) to be required, weekly reports were adopted after only 2 weeks of operation. It is likely that these will soon be replaced by monthly, quarterly, and in some cases even annual reports.

It is also important to observe in this regard that one type of report is prepared in present-day systems so that information explicitly contained in the files can be utilized by management for decisions guiding system response. Reports of this type do not require an appreciable amount of processing to produce but merely extract information—already contained in the files—for visual reference. The idea that such reports are really required in printed form by management, except perhaps at very long intervals of time, should now be subject to renewed scrutiny. If the corresponding information is now stored in the computer system and is available for more or less *ad hoc* inquiries by interested parties, the whole concept of management reports whose function it is to make a list of information accessible to the manager is suspect.

The trend which seems to be developing is that the management report of the future will take form in a highly condensed exception-type presentation of those conditions not dealt with as part of the mechanized system. Voluminous printed reports depicting the fact that things are fine or that anticipated deviations from the norm have occurred will become a remnant of the dim dark past of manual or punched card processing of business data. The need for such "reports" will be eliminated by the computer system. Instead, the information used to compile them will be retained by the machine so that it can be given the detailed clerical attention it requires in a manner compatible with the use of a large-scale computer system.

Cost as a basis for comparison

In order to express the usefulness of one particular set of data-handling equipment as compared with another particular set, the common denominator of cost is usually selected as the basis for comparison. Our purpose is, as the economist would say, to compare marginal cost with marginal utility.

Salaries of the personnel required, the purchase price or rental fee for computing equipment, desks, and other capital equipment, the cost of floor space, and a suitable overhead factor must be known. These more or less obvious costs might be characterized as "direct" or "positive" costs associated with a data processing system. It is in the area of utility values, or "negative costs," attributable to a particular data processing system that accounting rigor is often lost and where judgment based on experience must play an important part in costing the complete operation.

To estimate utility values, we deal with such questions as: What is the value to an organization of knowing an inventory position 4 days earlier than previously? Of having monthly, rather than quarterly, sales analyses? Or of meeting payroll on Tuesday rather than Friday following a particular closing date? Value judgments here are necessary in order to make possible a rational decision as to the proper level of expenditure for computing equipment to do the job. These values may indeed be of such a magnitude as to overshadow completely the direct costs incurred.

In many cases some considerable amount of time and expense must be associated just with arriving at the cost estimate described above. A lengthy procedural study is sometimes necessary even to estimate precisely the equipment required to do the job, although to some extent the definition of the details encompassed by the job is properly related to the equipment selected.

In a few isolated cases significant gains in data processing efficiency can obviously be achieved by substituting any of several sets of alternative data processing equipment for the present (presumably nonmechanized) system. It is possible that these gains will prove to be large and hence important. In such cases it is probably well to proceed with the acquisition of the arbitrarily selected new equipment and essentially "mechanize the present system" with it. This is done, of course, in the interest of realizing the expected important gains as soon as possible, and at the same time it saves most of the costs introduced by the usual feasibility study which precedes the installation of large-scale data processing equipment.

In those cases where the "arbitrary" equipment selection has been made, there remains the possibility of achieving substantial further system improvement by installing a really new data processing system based on new concepts of organization. These further gains are not likely to have been realized in the first change. They too may be large. A decision about further change remains to be made and the suggestion that a preferred system has been achieved must be rejected.

It would be grossly inaccurate for us to foster the idea that improvements in the efficiency of data processing in a given firm are the product solely of introducing improved data processing equipment. Indeed almost every example is in some way contrary to this idea. In apparently ordinary situations, systems studies designed to examine the presumed advantages of the installations of data processing equipment have revealed that as much as 80 per cent of the gain made possible by the equipment could be achieved without it. Usually this is done by an appropriate redesign of the manual procedures to correspond to the changes in business environment which have taken place since their original design. Even in those cases where data processing equipment offers the greatest advantage in business operations, improvements provided by the accompanying redesign of the remaining manual operations are usually an important contributor to the total improvement.

Yet there remains an important segment of data processing operations where our desire to introduce newly available techniques of scientific management and our need to handle ever-growing quantities of information in the course of our daily activities absolutely dictate the use of modern data processing equipment. It is to the growing incidence of such applications that this book is primarily dedicated.

In this discussion no mention has been made of any "excess" data processing capacity. A cost analysis is made entirely on the basis of the value to the company of jobs done, and the costs of doing them. Thus any work done utilizing excess capacity should have been considered as a part of this analysis and hence does not represent really excess capacity. It is essential to realize in this connection that it is not necessary or indeed even desirable to plan to utilize data-handling equipment to the limit of its capacity. In the first place there are rental, personnel, and overhead costs incurred in any extra shift operation, thus reducing the possibility of "free" products from the system. An even more important consideration, however, is that of providing sufficient slack time in a given time period to allow for such contingencies as peak loads, moderate increase in normal loads, development of new operations, a reasonable number of unforeseen special projects, and, finally, equipment unavailability due to engineering causes as well as errors committed by operating personnel. Here again only broad prior experience with these problems can hope to approximate realistically the proper unscheduled time which should be provided in a particular system.

Anomalies of an EDP system

The optimum use of EDP equipment of one sort or another as a major tool in a firm's data processing system usually implies a major change in the operating concept of the company itself. This may be true either because the different operating concept is *dictated* by the EDP equipment or because the means to improve the operating concept is *provided* by the same equipment. The former cause refers largely to increased rigor introduced into the system by the equipment, while the latter refers largely to the improved company operation expected to be provided by the

computer. The conceptual changes provided by EDP equipment are discussed elsewhere; let us consider some of the
changes dictated by the machines.

Perhaps the most important requirement imposed on a
firm by the introduction of EDP equipment into the data
processing activity is a new kind of expertness, that of the
"data processing specialist."

This man is not primarily a computer programmer although he must know computer programming, he is not
primarily an operations research specialist although he must
have an understanding of operations research, and he is not
primarily a computer designer or manufacturer although he
must be familiar with the problems and capabilities of the
computer designer and manufacturer. All these skills are
likely to be required for the introduction of a new data
processing system and they must be brought together for
one common purpose by a project leader cognizant of the
considerations involved. While he must have a real understanding of all the technical areas just mentioned, the really
new skill with which the data processing specialist is concerned is that of the operational impact of machines on
management of all levels, employees not directly concerned
with the machine, the computer operators themselves, and
perhaps the general public for certain firms. It is these man-
machine relationship problems which this specialist must
be prepared to solve.

Probably the first such problem to be faced is that of
establishing new concepts acceptable to management and
at the same time retaining potential machine benefits. To
a certain extent, this requires that EDP equipment be "sold"

to all levels of management. This involves an understanding of the limitations of an EDP system in the light of the benefits to be achieved. It may be that some data processing tasks cannot be accomplished as effectively with the new EDP system as they were with the former system, *according to the standards of the former system*. This suggests that a large-scale system is likely to involve a great many new standards of efficiency as compared with the system it replaces.

To the extent that new standards are involved, the sale of these standards must precede that of EDP equipment. In this way management acceptance of the procedures recommended for the EDP system is related to a common set of criteria for both the objectives of the firm and the requirements of the EDP equipment. Only by treating the hardware as part of a total system can a significant portion of the potential gains offered by a really new data processing system be achieved.

Because of this total system approach, based on newly developed criteria for company operation, it follows that a new "data processing" organization within the company probably must be established. While this organization is likely to include the technical skills associated with computer operation, its more important function is system design in the sense suggested on these pages.

It will almost certainly be the case that the new system will be more complex than the old. This poses problems the only solution to which is an awareness of their existence and a readiness to cope with them as they arise. The essence of these problems is that it is probably impossible for one man to be cognizant at any given time of all the complex interrelations of the functions involved. A competent staff, of course, can help, but certain other after-the-fact steps must be provided for. These arise from periodic reviews, during the development period, of the whole EDP system against the accepted operating criteria. Expansions of and additions to the system are likely to be indicated. Corresponding increases to the data processing staff and increased development costs due to a variety of other causes may occur during the development period. Failure to expect and provide generally for such unknowns may lead to the failure to develop a system of the capability otherwise possible.

Partly because of the complexity mentioned above, the system development time will almost surely be longer than one might think. System expansion and changes during the development period are obvious causes of this. The time required for shakedown of the machine operations (often called "debugging time") plus that required for the total system shakedown is typically much more than that required for a manual or punched card system, the essence of which is simply to improve or mechanize the firm's paperwork operations. Here again expandability of the system development operation, this time in terms of completion date, must be provided for in the initial planning. Refusal to undertake this slippage in the development schedule may cause the EDP system unnecessarily to miss the otherwise attainable mark of effectiveness.

In some respects, the correctness of the information with which the EDP system deals presents a situation peculiar to the use of EDP equipment. The problem of accurate processing of information and hence of the production of accurate results and reports is of course present and in most ways conceptually similar to the same problem in any other kind of data processing system. Additions and multiplications must be made correctly and the means for an appropriate degree of accuracy evaluation must be provided. There is, however, a major difference between the accuracy controls which are part of an EDP system and those which are part of a manual one. This difference is essentially that accuracy controls in the new system must be an integral part of the system rather than an after-the-fact operation. Separate large volume and complex corrective actions by either people or machines must be eliminated by the system design. The reason for this is patent. The EDP system is a high-speed large-volume operation the very complexity and integrated nature of which implies that the propagation of errors over the entire data processing system will occur very rapidly.

The problem of correcting errors produced by the machines themselves is fortunately quite small, owing in part to the inherent accuracy of machine processing and in part to the extensive opportunities automatically to detect machine errors. But errors of either fact or format in information presented by *people* for processing by machine introduce a far larger problem, primarily because their number is likely to be much greater than the number of machine errors, since they involve operations by people. The data processing operation itself must be so designed that it will correct these errors wherever possible or, in the absence of the information necessary for such correction, ensure that the input item in error is detected, not entered into the system, and rerouted for local or source correction. The major incompatibility between the rate at which errors and their propagation can be corrected after they once enter the system and the rate at which processing is done by the equipment dictates the absolute necessity to minimize the entry of errors into the system and their generation therein. To this end, in a typical application, the first 20 per cent of the machine steps executed are concerned entirely with detection and correction of input errors, while 50 per cent of the remaining machine program deals with detection and correction of similar errors and of operations which may have been carried out incorrectly by the machine.

Flexibility of operating schedule is a further requirement of a successful EDP system. As a direct result of the high-speed large-volume character of the system, mentioned above, work stoppages due to causes which cannot be specifically predicted produce a greater impact on the system than would similar stoppages in a slower-speed less-integrated operation. Errors in input information, in spite of the precautions discussed above, remain an important cause for such stoppages. And, although the computer specialist may be reluctant to admit it, recent history reveals that machine failures still represent a significant cause of the interruption of work progress in a system in which a computer is an integral part.

Since these stoppages are by definition unpredictable, the particular means to cope with the "next" stoppage cannot be known. In general it is obvious that a certain amount of slack time must be provided for this purpose. The exact amount cannot even be suggested out of context with the particular system and in context is at best an estimate. An effort as a part of the system development to identify as many as possible of the causes for system stoppages, together with the means for dealing with them, should prove helpful. The capability to provide fast efficient machine maintenance, often on the part of the manufacturer, is an important factor in this regard. Failure to interpret properly the expected machine "down" time could represent (and has represented) an important element in the failure of an EDP system to achieve the expected result.

While the so-called "large-scale general-purpose" computers of today are typically subject to one or two failures of a few minutes' duration each day (and occasionally fall prey to much more serious engineering difficulties), certain special-purpose digital computers presently in use exhibit a much better record. Computers used at race tracks to accumulate on a continuous basis the dollar totals bet are known to have had no failure requiring over about 6 minutes to repair over a period of many years. By employing engineering components considered antiquated in the general-purpose computer field and by the continuous use of highly trained maintenance technicians, these "race-track computers" have achieved the degree of reliability requisite to their use in a somewhat tense environment of man-machine relationships.

Finally, a crucial difficulty identified only recently is somewhat more subtle and will perhaps prove to be more important in the operation of large systems than those mentioned previously. It is simply this: As the computer system becomes faster and larger, and consequently the details of the information processing operations become increasingly included as parts of the mechanized EDP system, people—operators and supervisors as well as managers—tend to lose their capability to know, at any given time, the exact status of the data processing operation.

This means that, at the time of a temporary unavailability of the equipment due to machine failure or other causes, the people involved will not be cognizant of the information (describing the current situation) necessary for them to carry out manually the data processing operations during the remainder of the unavailability period. It further implies that, even when all the equipment is available as intended by the system planners, the tremendous complexity of the system operation will produce and cope with involved situations too rapidly to allow comprehension by the human components of the system. To restate: Increased use of systems based on computers and associated equipment will create situations where complex events are taking place under computer control at a rate which is much too fast for the human supervisor to follow and with a complexity which may extend even beyond that specifically anticipated by the system designer (although never beyond that implicitly provided for).

The above considerations suggest that the very great disparity between the capacity of mechanized and human data processors to deal rapidly and in large volume with a great many types of information bearing on a particular decision may establish the fundamental limit in extending

EDP applications into the field of commercial data processing. Although the state of the art of application of this equipment to business problems is not crowding this fundamental limitation, it is highly probable that this failure of cognizance on the part of the people on behalf of whom the computer is performing will provide a kind of sociological ceiling of such significance that it must be considered in planning for integrated EDP systems taking place even in today's environment.

Some examples of this phenomenon are of interest.

The establishment of air traffic control networks employing digital computers presents an almost classic situation, with the very reason for the system development at the focal point of the problem. The obviously rapid growth of air traffic and the consequent need for central ground control of that traffic created a problem too complex and voluminous for people practically to handle. The problem involves the efficient scheduling of landings, take-offs, and in-flight maneuvers to minimize the danger involved in the vicinity of the large airports of today.

One of the worst such situations exists in the New York City area where the four large airports served in 1957 about 2,000 flights daily within a radius of only 12 miles. The assignment of the problem of controlling these flights to a large-scale computer system for automated handling creates the following situation: the computer system deals effectively with a great many details pertaining to the control of this traffic—such as the number of aircraft awaiting instructions, how far they are from their destination, their fuel situation, and the queue at each terminal—and determines the optimum solution to the problem on a continuous basis based on all the relevant data. In the event that the computer must be removed from the system and the operation carried out manually, the people who would then be required to solve the problem must at once become aware of a great many facts of which only the computer was previously "aware." They have not had the chance to build the fund of knowledge possessed by the computer and, in fact, if it were practical for them to have done this there would not have been the need for the computer in the first place.

The ability of a computer to deal with highly complex situations in "real time" and the concomitant danger of un-scheduled unavailability of the computer during normally operational periods is a fundamental problem in this type of application. Although significant strides have been taken toward solution by increasing equipment reliability and standby capacity, no panacea has been developed and none seems likely in the foreseeable future.

Unfortunately, people have a tendency not to take their limitations seriously. Their attitude seems to be that "people are better than anybody." This is true in most cases in point of creative design or original thinking (whatever you care to call it), but it is certainly false as regards effective operation of an existing data processing system. Just as it would not be feasible for an engineer to design and build a modern motor car or airplane without prior knowledge of the art, so it is not possible for the personnel concerned with the operation of a modern EDP system to comprehend at once the data processing situation as depicted and "understood" by the computer.

In a great many cases, the need (real or apparent) to provide alternate procedures in the event of a system failure remains an unsolved problem. Machine stops for any reason whatever create a corresponding delay of the data processing activity. In most cases no attempt is made to carry on manually until repairs can be made, but rather the procedure is simply to wait until the equipment can be made operative. Such delays are unsatisfactory in those cases where the operation of the afflicted equipment is intended to correspond directly with second-by-second or minute-by-minute operations of the environment itself.

Since delays due to system failures cannot be eliminated altogether in any case, it is pertinent to discuss ways to reduce the inconvenience they cause. The first is to avoid, if at all possible, the introduction of these so-called "on-line" operations into the system. The suggestion of such a thing, of course, generates major opposition, primarily on the part of management. The argument, "We cannot eliminate this on-line operation since the system must provide 'at least' all the capabilities we formerly had in our manual system" is often heard. Such an argument is often invalid. The only way rationally to resolve the question is to compare the old on-line operations with the alternatives offered by the new EDP system *in the light of the new criteria* developed for the firm's data processing function. It is not our intention to depreciate the task of convincing management that such a decision process is preferred but merely to suggest that it is. The widespread acceptance of large-scale EDP systems as a completely new way of life, so to speak, for a business, will evolve only as a result of unrelenting effort on the part of the data processing specialists to produce these systems and from their successful demonstration over a period of many years.

For those systems remaining where on-line operation is judged to be an essential part of the system in the final analysis, certain rather unsophisticated measures can be taken to provide continued operational ability in the event of machine failure. Because the basic file records are presumably part of the machine system, auxiliary means for obtaining access to these records can be provided toward this end.

If the normal means of access are unavailable, particular information from the large file, stored magnetically on such media as cards, tapes, drums or disks, can be referred to by special inquiry devices and printed, punched, or otherwise displayed for visual access. Even though the reference itself is automatic, it is likely to involve manual operations such as keying input information, mounting the storage media on appropriate transport devices, and depressing appropriate buttons or switches. These operations occur at a much slower rate than the corresponding operations performed automatically by the EDP equipment. In addition, since we have assumed that the central processor is unavailable, the required processing is necessarily manual in this situation.

Alternatively, in anticipation of this situation, a printed record of a selected portion of the pertinent information in the automatic file can be produced periodically for use when automatic access to the file cannot be obtained through the usual channels. Either of these procedures is a relatively (and approximately equally) tedious method of coping manually with the problem of the unavailability of equipment, intended to be used on-line with company operations which by definition cannot be handled automatically.

In those cases where the computers are used for periodic processing, small delays may be quite inconsequential. When an unavoidable delay is long enough to be troublesome, standby procedures can often be employed. For really extended periods of trouble, the use of similar equipment located in a nearby firm or in a service bureau has often been provided for.

The foregoing discussion provides an excellent example of an aspect of system design which may be dictated by equipment considerations. While the final decision as to the precise procedures to be employed must be made within the context of a particular problem, the suggestion that certain underlying constraints are introduced by the equipment employed should be evident.

Long- and short-range planning

From time to time the "experts" in the field of electronic data processing debate the question of whether the long-range planning approach is superior to that of the immediate direct cost benefit (we use this term for want of any more widely accepted one), or vice versa. These debates ostensibly deal with the real problem of whether to strive for immediate relief from current difficulties in data processing or to attempt to achieve larger benefits over a longer run. Such debates are invariably held out of context with any applications of computers to which they may be applied in the *future,* although *past* applications are often used as "examples" to lend credence to the particular conclusion reached. For this reason, they fail in their objective to choose between a long- and short-range plan.

The fallacy underlying such an approach has already been suggested in the earlier pages of this book: Whether long-range benefits are preferable alternatives to short-range benefits or not depends almost entirely on the fundamental objectives that top management seeks to achieve, all things considered! Hence these objectives must be identified before a choice can be made. Since this statement is rather broad and all-encompassing, let us examine it further to determine its significance when a particular environment is specified.

The subject of the present controversy can probably be stated in a more precise manner than above (the above form was used since it probably gains in familiarity what it lacks in precision). In spite of an almost universal failure to do so, there seems to be no reasonable basis on which to question the position that one should begin the planning of a system by identifying those goals which he judges to be both attainable and most nearly optimal. As a criterion against which to judge results, he must select a unit of measure (dollars, happy employees) and a unit of time (days, decades) at the end of which he wishes to maximize this measure.

With these selections made, this planner is not only in an excellent position to proceed, but he will very likely find that he is prepared to select a particular course of action (long or short in range) without an appreciable amount of further work.

Consider some examples of such an approach. The planner may have decided that his objective for this particular plan is to maximize his profits over the next 10 months. Alternatively, it may have become apparent that the most desirable objective is to strive for incentive, security, and the physical and financial well-being of the employees in the factory (or of top management) over a much longer period of time.

Having decided upon a set of goals which are both obtainable and most nearly optimal, the planner (management) can now select a set of related lesser goals, ranked in order of preference, in a similar manner. The important thing now is to make certain that these subsidiary goals are truly compatible with each other and with the primary goal named. Thus, if the primary goal is to achieve the best competitive position in a particular industry at the end of 5 years, it may be quite inconsistent to attempt to maximize the profits of the next 10 months.

At the point where these goals have been established, it is almost invariably true that any choice between long- and short-range planning has resolved itself. Consider an example: The goal of maximizing one's competitive position at the end of 5 years has been selected; it has been determined that such a goal will necessarily involve large dollar expenditures for research during the intervening years with corresponding reduced profits to the stockholders in that period. In such a situation, the decision that the primary goal is to satisfy the stockholders *from year to year* will dictate that this relatively long-range plan must be abandoned in favor of a much shorter range plan which will (presumably) provide more immediate (although not necessarily more lasting) profits.

Returning now specifically to the "choice" between long- and short-range planning, the situation can be seen to have taken on a somewhat different light. It is assumed at the very beginning that planning for the short range will provide greater advantages (profits) or other management objectives *in the short range* than will long-range planning. We seek now to specify a plan which will offer, according to our estimate, the greatest advantage to our organization in terms of its objectives by the end of a specified period and thereafter, that is, a plan which will provide us with the most favorable *cumulative* position *by and after a specified point in time*. When this period is long, as compared with the period for the short-range plan mentioned above, such a plan is said to be a long-range plan.

In the course of specifying this long-range plan it will be necessary to reexamine the original objectives in order to determine whether the difficulties which would be encountered during the implementation of the plan violate organizational dicta actually less flexible than the objectives we have said we are seeking to achieve. One example of such a problem is the possibility of sharply decreased net profits during the period preceding the time when the long-range plan is expected to bear its fruit. Another such example is the possibility of abrupt, awkward, and costly personnel problems introduced by the instigation of a sharply discontinuous set of company procedures attendant to highly visionary long-range planning. While it is obvious that a well-designed long-range plan will seek as an integral part of the plan to minimize these difficulties, a reappraisal may reveal that a significant portion of them remain.

When the systems planner has proceeded as above, he may be able to describe a long-range plan which does indeed provide his firm with the most favorable cumulative position by the end of a specified time and thereafter, which achieves those objectives which he still believes to be primary, and which does all this without violating rigid company rules or personal mores. If we can specify such a plan, surely we have proved the course of the "long-range plan" as superior in every way to that of the shorter one. Failing any of these, it seems clear that striving for the shorter-range objectives is the better course of action.

We believe that the above discussion demonstrates conclusively that it is not results experienced in the past which should govern our planning concept. Rather, the planning concept employed must be based on a careful consideration and reconsideration of the goals we truly seek to achieve for the future and the pitfalls we are likely to encounter en route. This, in the light of a realistic estimate of the potentialities of the data processing systems proposed, will enable the planner to select that system most appropriate for the particular situation he has encountered.

CHAPTER 5

Decision Making

DECISION MAKING is an activity which has historically been performed by people. These people, including you and me, seem rather defensive about their exclusive prerogatives to perform this activity, that is, their prerogatives to "make decisions." To suggest that some inanimate object like a digital computer will soon be "able" (or is presently "able") to make decisions previously made by people is damaging to the ego and thus constitutes a major form of heresy.

Nevertheless this suggestion has been made and is discussed on the following pages. The capability of the digital computer to make decisions has often been described as one of the fundamental characteristics of the set of equipment which constitutes a digital computer system. While some of this description has been factual and some admittedly fictional, the concept of automatic decision making has become inseparable from that of computers in the minds of most.

A definition of decision making

The process by which one arrives at conclusions—makes decisions—is interesting to examine. In the first place, while these conclusions are usually said to derive directly from a set of "facts," it almost always develops that these so-called "facts" are in reality an *estimate* of the true facts of the case, made from as many clues as are available to the estimator.

The question now arises as to whether the available clues have been dealt with systematically and logically, are of sufficient scope to provide the basis for a decision, and do not distort the facts (as clues in detective stories so often do). One may think of this situation as a competition between Life and the decision maker, wherein the role of Life is to choose the underlying state of things, and the role of the decision maker is to select an action dependent upon the strategy of Life and at the same time most favorable to himself.

In order to perform his function in a business environment, the decision maker often employs relatively costly data processing techniques and equipment. By utilizing these facilities, he then hopes to obtain some information about the strategy which has been selected by Life. In theory this information can be improved (up to a limit) by increased processing of more and more data toward this end.

As a balancing factor, however, there are (sometimes rather major) costs associated with this processing. The problem now becomes that of balancing the cost of data processing against the cost of errors in decision making (which could potentially be lowered if more processing were carried out as a result of more money's being spent for this purpose).

Finally, the decision maker must decide whether even all the data theoretically available and completely processed can guarantee accurate decisions. This is not possible, for example, if the decision involves such fundamental uncertainties as whether past history will prove to be representative of future events in general and, moreover, the particular future events about which he must decide. We have come to expect the sun unfailingly to rise each morning and to set each evening and it is highly probable that it will do so tomorrow; but it is *not certain* it will! It is substantially less certain that our boss will continue to operate our organization as stubbornly and improperly as he has in the past, although the history of the situation certainly suggests he will do so.

Decision making, then, is the job of determining the course of action which is most likely to produce the desired results according to some predetermined criteria. When the criteria and the rules for determining likeliness are explicitly provided to a device, such as a digital computer, which has the capability to manipulate this information logically, the computer assumes the ability to process data according to these criteria and rules, and hence to "make decisions."

Elements of decision making

Decision making can theoretically be carried out according to a systematic logical plan. It is in such cases called "scientific decision making." Scientific decision making by numerical means may involve techniques from the fields of mathematical statistics, information theory, logical nets, symbolic logic, game theory, linear programming, and dynamic programming. Decisions made by the proper application of these techniques are by definition "correct," since the fields themselves can be shown to be internally consistent and completely determinate.

For this reason, scientific decision making by the use of a digital computer "simplifies" to the problem of the proper application of the techniques mentioned above. While this is not a simple problem in the sense that every man on the street is completely conversant with the application of these techniques, their application is well defined to the experts. Once the problem has been represented mathematically, its solution becomes a relatively simple problem for the trained technician.

But the major difficulty remains. It is the fundamental requirement to reflect properly in mathematical terms the real problem encountered so that the mathematical decision, when made, does represent the solution to the original problem. In a great many cases, this difficulty is absolutely impossible to overcome!

There are a great many reasons for this, a complete discussion of which is beyond the scope of this book. A list of some of the more common of these reasons includes:

1. The persons versed in the science of the mathematical representation of problems are usually unversed in the art of understanding the basic nature of the undefined problems they encounter.

2. The people to whom the problems belong are without an airtight logical definition of them—business problems have often been developed rather intuitively over long

periods of time by a great many people and hence do not emerge as well-defined systems.

3. Nonmathematical ("human") considerations—don't fire that man, his wife twisted her ankle last week while bowling with the company bowling team—are often present and sometimes completely dominate the decision made.

4. The data used to develop the equations intended to define the decision rules often fail to constitute a representative sample of the total information generated.

5. The data used in the solution have been incompletely and/or inaccurately gathered—here we have one of the major sources of difficulty since the people who are assigned to enter data into the system (make out receipts by repairmen, time charges by mechanics) are not so immediately concerned with the effective operation of the system as with getting their own job of salesman, warehouseman, or mechanic completed quickly and properly.

In the past few decades there has been a considerable amount of study in the field of decision theory. A great many names have been associated with these studies. It is of interest to study the decisions with which this theory is concerned since they are logically quite similar to decisions in those business situations which are well defined. Even though, as pointed out above, it is not the usual case that business situations are well defined, the role of the decision maker is to assume that the definition he is given is in fact correct. Concern about the gulf between the definition of the problem which he is given and the true nature of the problem is not properly that of the decision maker (at least not in his role as decision maker). By approaching the problem in this way, the decision maker is able to place his problem in one-to-one correspondence with that represented by this theory and so to employ techniques developed for solution to "gaming" problems in the solution of his problems of the "real world."

Most of the theoretical work which has been done in the field of decision theory has dealt with problems of a determinable nature. Thus the reasoning involved in playing nim, checkers, chess, contract bridge, and several other games has been explored. While nim and, to a lesser extent, checkers are simple games, the other games mentioned are so complex that, even though they are determinable, i.e., a satisfactory solution can be drawn from a finite number of possibilities, this number is so large that it has so far been considered infinite.

Although the possible logical paths leading to a solution to these games are very many indeed, the rules involved are often quite simple. This is equivalent to saying that the mathematics (logic) defining the *rules* of these games is simple but that the mathematics describing a preferred *application* of the rules in order to obtain an optimal solution is very complex indeed.

A digital computer is a device with a considerable facility to manipulate (add, subtract, multiply, divide, compare, etc.) numbers and thus with some facility to apply these rules. Let us consider, as Bowden did,[1] whether it is theoretically possible to build a digital computer which could:

---

[1] These considerations are similar to those found in *Faster Than Thought*, edited by Bowden, Sir Isaac Pitman & Sons, Ltd., London, 1955.

1. Perform its activities within the rules of the game and identify any activities outside the legal limits of the rules

2. Solve problems of limited scope within the rules of a game (as, for example, to indicate whether, in a given position in a chess game, white has forced mate in three or to indicate whether, for a particular deal of hands in contract bridge, a given sequence of play will or will not make the given contract)

3. Play a reasonably good game of chess (bridge), i.e., given any chess (bridge) situation which is not particularly unusual or difficult, indicate a reasonably good move (play) after several minutes of computer calculation toward that end

4. Play chess or contract bridge, as defined above, and improve its play from game to game, profiting in each game by the experience gained in the previous games

5. Answer questions put to it so that it is not possible for the questioner (if he cannot see the machine) to determine whether the answers given are those of a man or of the machine, i.e., give an appropriate number of wrong, partially wrong, or misleading answers

6. Respond to any situation with conclusions based on feelings, biases, intuition, and other reactions familiar to the psychologist, just as man does

The science-fiction writer is way ahead of this writer; he has said for many years that all this can readily be done, although it may take a few years to implement. In most cases, he is probably closer to being correct than one might think he is.

The reader can readily see how (1) can be accomplished by a computer. After all, there are really very few rules to deal with. Likewise, (2) is almost as easy to accomplish since—in chess or bridge—even all the possibilities made available by this limited subset of the total game does not represent a very large number of possibilities.

To play a reasonably good game, (3) is also rather clearly possible, although somewhat more difficult. It is possible partly because we usually mean by "reasonably good" that the player (computer) must win only about half the games against another player of average ability and, moreover, in order to do this it need not make the optimal play at every turn since it will have ample opportunity to recover from a reasonable number of errors in play and to take advantage of a similar number of errors made by its human opponent.

The question becomes slightly more sticky when we come to consider (4), which really amounts to learning, at least as far as chess or contract bridge is concerned. Although it is intuitively very difficult to accept the fact that a computer is capable of learning in a sense which is quite real, it must be remembered that the scope of learning suggested here is extremely narrow (being limited to the single subject of, say, chess) as compared with the normal scope of human learning. The digital computer is therefore certainly capable of recording in its memory events which have occurred in past games, searching through this memory to find already proved solutions to situations similar to those now confronting it, and even of erasing the record of a problem solved ("forgetting") when it has been unused for some time and the space in which the record is stored is now required for the record of some recent event. In the course of such an endeavor, the computer now begins to face limitations imposed by storage access time or storage size which tend to bind its effectiveness in the field of learning. These limits are advancing at a rapid rate along with the general state of the art of digital computers. Even today, computers are able to play the game of chess on a par with players of considerable skill, beating them a reasonable number of times and playing very rapidly indeed. This "ability," to be sure, is a clever definition of the problem by omnipotent man to the computer doing the job.

The problem of building a computer and programming it so that it will *appear* to think like a man (5) is considerably broader in scope than that of playing a proper game of chess. But it is probably logically identical. A great many facts must be available to the computer to accomplish this, and it must be able to retrieve them very rapidly and manipulate them logically according to modes of reasoning (logic) selected from a large set of logical alternatives. While such a computer is surely out of the question even at the level of today's research, it would seem overly pessimistic to suppose that it will never be possible to build one.

One question (6) then remains: Is it theoretically possible to build a computer which will respond to any situation with conclusions based on feelings, biases, and intuition, even as you and I. This is, as Bowden points out, something I can never know, just as I do not know whether *you* respond to situations with conclusions based on feelings, biases, and intuition, as I do. It seems possible to take a more optimistic point of view on this question than Bowden suggests; namely, studies currently under way in the theory of complex information processing may reveal that the fundamental nature of intellectual response in people is such as to permit us in the far distant future to duplicate these processes on a very large, very fast digital computer.

Complex information processing as a tool in decision making

Most problems which deserve to be called "complex" are characterized by the dual facts that the processing required to solve them cannot be known until some processing is completed and that a solution to each such problem is required within a limited amount of time. In addition, they appear to be characterized in varying degrees by a nearly inexhaustible amount of information relevant to their solution and by the existence of an extremely large set of potential solutions.

These characteristics of complex problems immediately suggest that a computer capable of solving them must be able to solve any set of logical equations and be able to solve them so fast that the degree of their complexity is usually of minor consequence. But this is useful only when some entity (human or machine) understands the particular problem sufficiently well to describe it in detail, i.e., write the logical equations theoretically sufficient for its solution. This last requirement cannot always be met.

Decisions are easily made when the alternatives and all their ramifications are unambiguously presented and when all the necessary data are available. The fact that different people decide different things in the same situation (and even that the same people decide different things faced with the same situation at different times) seems certainly to indicate that not all the data and possible alternative decisions and decision criteria are available to each person.

The human approach to this difficulty is to approximate the optimal solution as described above by the simple device of *continuous human cognizance* as the solution proceeds, i.e., continuous redefinition of the problem and the consequent identification of alternate possible solutions, and introduction of new data as they become available. Such an approach recognizes the problem as one having different forms at different stages, and the path to the optimal solution as one found by testing and trying many different solutions at each point of decision.

Developments are in process today which will enable a digital computer to make step-by-step decisions in these heteromorphic problems by such probative means. This is done by eliminating from further consideration at each step those alternatives which, on the basis of the information available at that point, have the lowest probability of being the most favorable alternative. This is done until the number of remaining alternatives is sufficiently small to enable the computer to deal logically with them. While the exact number of alternatives which can be dealt with on a logical basis is of course a function of the size of the information storage of the computer and of its speed, the number often proves to be sufficient to make "good" decisions. Thus the computer can approach the solution of a problem exactly the same as problem solvers do; i.e., neither computers nor people always have available a complete set of data and alternative decisions at every given decision point. The difference is a matter of degree.

This point can be illustrated by an example in the field of programming a digital computer to play chess. On the basis of the rules and objectives of the game and values assigned for each piece, the computer assumes the role of a player.

First it is necessary to define the basic rules of the game in a form which can be interpreted by the computer. Such a form is the computer program, a sequence of coded instructions to the computer. In our example, this portion of the program enables the computer to solve the set of mathematical equations which reflect these rules.

Next we assign a quantity to each chess piece. Such quantities enable the computer to "know," for example, that a queen is worth more than a bishop and so should be protected more zealously. It is often desirable to assign a whole set of quantities to each piece so that their changing worth as the game progresses can be accounted for.

Finally, the objectives of the game are defined in terms of the computer program, again as a sequence of coded instructions which represent a set of mathematical equations. Thus the computer "knows" that an objective is to capture its opponent's bishop, but not at the loss of a queen, and ultimately to capture the opponent's king. This portion of the program, when executed, provides the computer with a set of values against which it can measure its situation at any point in the game, or by means of which it can project its situation into the future. It is clear that no statement of these values can be exhaustive in the game of chess because there are just too many possibilities, but the incomplete statement that can be provided has proved sufficient to do a remarkable job of playing the game.

The computer is now ready to begin play. Its moves and those of its opponent (which may, incidentally, be another computer) occur alternately, the computer "deciding" on its own moves by solving the logical equations of which its program consists and making each solution known to the operator, and the moves of its opponent being indicated, in turn, to the computer. At each turn, the computer computes a value for a group of alternative moves according to the value scale which it has been given and selects the move with the highest value. This sequence of events proceeds until the game has been completed.

At the same time that it is deciding on its moves for the present game, the computer is recording in its memory the effects which it "experiences" from the moves it makes, again according to the same scale of values. Thus it is accumulating experience. As the amount of experience accumulated increases, as each move must be made the program directs the computer to search its memory for situations which it has already experienced which are similar to the present one, rather than to compute anew a value for several of the possible moves available to it. In this way, the number of alternative moves available to the computer increases substantially as it plays more games, much in the same way as people gain experience by repeated play.

Eventually, however, either the computer storage is

filled or the amount of time required to search the storage to review all the experience stored there becomes excessively great. At this time, instead of simply ceasing to collect experience, the computer program can direct the computer to discard the experience which it uses most infrequently whenever it can substitute more pertinent experience in its stead. This corresponds to forgetting in human beings and, because the computer "forgets" according to plan, may even prove to be a more organized form of forgetting than that of which people are capable.

It is noteworthy that a computer has actually been programmed to play checkers in an analogous manner and has demonstrated a rather good game. This, then, is truly an example of complex information processing by means of a digital computer. Over a group of games the processing is heteromorphic and the method employed probative. The computer wins and loses, much the same as a man would do (although it is not likely to lose twice in exactly the same way). It seems already to have achieved a "human" solution to a problem in complex information processing.

When digital computers were first introduced commercially, after World War II, many of the designers were very vocal in proclaiming vast capabilities for the machines with respect to imitation of human thought (thereby suggesting the name "brain" for the machines) by the machine as a whole and even by its individual components. But before the middle of the next decade the pendulum had swung the other way and the more vocal of the so-called "experts" seemed to be those who were denouncing the preeminence of the computer as a thinker and relegating it to the accomplishment of only routine tasks. When, in 1949, E. C. Berkeley published *Giant Brains*,[2] most computer experts of the day cringed at the choice of words.

Now we can detect a growing tendency to regard digital computers as devices capable of carrying out deductive thought processes. Considerable evidence exists to support this new attitude. This approach to the problem departs from the idea that computers are fast and dumb devices, and considers that they, in combination with their programs, may be more "logical" than people and, in addition, that they can go to places (such as the moon, planets, or radioactive areas on earth) where people cannot go and hence offer a means of locating logic in such places.

The evidence in this field of complex information processing can be divided into three kinds: discoveries about the nature of thought processes, i.e., how human thought processes are carried out; computer programs which make machines behave intelligently, i.e., play master chess, abstract an article and produce a real and useful summary of it, prove mathematical theorems, and perform routine mathematical analysis at the college level; and new concepts for communication by people to machines, i.e., computer programming.

A list of some of the key developments in the field includes:

1955: Selfridge and Deneen; Lincoln Labs. A computer program that attempted actually to learn visual patterns. It was successful in distinguishing between patterns and

---

[2] Edmund C. Berkeley, *Giant Brains*, John Wiley & Sons, New York, 1949.

not patterns, but not in distinguishing between triangles and squares.

1955: Samuel; IBM. A computer program to play checkers and improve its game with experience.

1956: Newell, Simon, and Shaw; the RAND Corporation. The Logic Theorist. A computer program which has successfully proved about three hundred theorems in logic.

1957: Bernstein; IBM. A chess program which enabled a computer successfully to defeat an inexperienced human player.

1958: Newell, Simon, and Shaw; The RAND Corporation. A more sophisticated chess program.

1958: Gelernter; IBM. A program to prove theorems in plane geometry is in development.

1958: Newell, Simon, and Shaw; The RAND Corporation. A General Problem Solving Program made up of two parts, the first of which contains the logic for general problem solving (within the scope covered), and the second of which contains the rules for a particular subject matter, e.g., symbolic logic, trigonometric identities, integration, plane geometry, or chess. Together these parts will be able to solve problems within a particular subject matter.

1958: Newell. Empirical research in cognitive human thought processes.

It remains a philosophical or semantic question whether problem solving of this kind performed on computers actually constitutes "thinking" by the machine. Proponents of this point of view contend that, since a knowledge of the program which was designed by human beings only theoretically enables these human beings to predict the process by which the problem will be solved by the computer, it is the machine and not the human which is capable of executing the theory and hence it might be said to be "thinking." The evidence, especially that cited above, offers some support for this view.

Data for decisions

Common to both human and machine solutions to problems of the real world is the need for decisions to be based on accurate data. Here again we face a difficult problem and indeed it is extremely rare if accurate data are in fact used as a basis for decisions. The reasons for this anomaly, discussed elsewhere in this book, include lack of controls for accuracy and completeness as an integral part of the system designed to collect the data, failure of the people involved to understand the importance and basic integrity of each piece of datum entered into the system, and finally just plain unavailability of the information required.

But while the reasons for bad data are fairly well known, a willingness to eradicate the cause of them is generally lacking in terms of time, personnel assignments, dollars expended for the purpose, and a generally strong attitude in support of an eradication effort. This seems at least partly due to a lack of a complete understanding of the impact of bad data on the entire system.

Any decision-making process can be described in terms of data collection, information processing, and decision making. It is evident again from such a description that data reflecting events and objectives are the basis for all decisions made. More specifically, the decision-making process of a data processing system consists of:

1. Data generation and introduction
   a. Instrumentation for recording of events
   b. Written forms for recording of events
   c. Selecting the proper description of the problem
2. Information processing
   a. Solving equations
   b. Detecting discrepancies from plan
   c. Summarizing and organizing data
3. Decision making
   a. In operating situations
   b. For planning purposes

The digital computer can be most active in the information processing phase of this process. It can, as has been described throughout the pages of this book, be operated so that it is faster, more comprehensive in scope, and more accurate than any person or group of people can possibly be. We have just discussed, furthermore, how the digital computer is becoming increasingly effective in making decisions based on results of these processing activities. It is of fundamental importance, however, that the value of processing, and decision making based on the results thereof, is entirely dependent on the data; no improvement which can be introduced by digital computers in these areas can overcome the inaccuracies or incompleteness of the data. Failure to introduce good data into the calculations can result only in the more rapid production of worthless results.

In a way this is an advantage, for the converse is also true. When a digital computer system is employed, we can be sure that the data entered have been correctly processed and that the decisions have been made according to the proper logical considerations. Thus errors in results can be almost definitely attributed either to data which fail properly to report events which have taken place in the system or to the inadequacy of rules by which these data are intended to be processed.

It can also be easier to detect errors in such systems. This can result, for example, if the calculations are made within the day or within the hour by the computer, rather than within the week or within the month by a group of people. In such a case, any pertinent omissions of data or calculated results identifiably out of bounds will be immediately apparent and can be returned to the originator of the data for correction. This can be most effective when done before the originator has forgotten the transaction or been otherwise diverted from the task of correcting data deficiencies for which he is responsible.

The combination of these two facts—that computer system errors are more easily identifiable with data and that they are more readily detected than those committed in less rigorous systems—has led to the common belief that errors are common in computer systems. A moment's reflection will reveal that just the reverse is true. It has been shown quantitatively that complex systems operating prior to the electronic data processing era were far less accurate, in terms of processing and decision making as well as data generation and introduction, than digital computer centered systems. That the error in data has taken on the role of the chief villain in the later system seems clearly due to the almost total elimination of the other errors so common in the older systems with which we are traditionally familiar.

The point of previous paragraphs then is that, while decisions are without question no better than the data on which they are based, they are quite likely to be as good in a system wherein processing and decisions are made by a digital computer, and they are almost sure to lose something in any translation by manual means.

Digital computers as processors of data can in many situations make available still another kind of advantage over slower systems with respect to the data they process: they can process a greater quantity and scope of relevant data in a given space of time and hence permit a more nearly accurate picture of the situation to be portrayed. It is obvious, for example, that the analysis of a sample consisting of 25,000 payments to a nationwide credit organization would be far more satisfactory statistically (and intuitively, for that matter) in revealing the payment pattern than an analysis of the 1,500 or 2,000 payments to which such samples are often limited.

Other developments in the recent past have revealed a further need for complex action and very high speed reaction. For example, military aircraft, with their complex navigational and fire-control systems, require the almost instantaneous reaction (decision) of the pilot in extremely complex situations represented by large amounts of data. Without the assistance of a digital computer to make these decisions—change the course of the aircraft or fire the rockets at the proper time—they would represent little more than guesses on the part of the pilot. In the future, the processing of the vast amounts of data required for control of manned satellites or rockets to the moon and planets is most certainly out of the question without a big assist from a digital computer assigned to the problem.

Humanism in decision making

Wherever digital computers are dealing with people and making decisions for them, and especially as these decisions are broad of scope rather than the results of the application of logically simple rules to the data at hand, it becomes necessary to provide the means for human intervention to ensure that the "human elements" of the decision have been properly taken into account. Whenever machines assume even a part of the decision-making job, the job of providing incentives for such things as accuracy, diligence, and general expertness of the people who are retained becomes acute.

Earlier in this chapter we have suggested a great many reasons why decisions can or should be made by computers. We now propose to discuss, briefly, some limitations imposed by the necessity to take into account the biases, habits, prejudices, and illogicalness of the people for whom the decisions are made and of those who must react to them.

Let us note at once that we do not intend to suggest that to have these biases, habits, prejudices, or even the illogicalness is wrong; rather our intent is simply to recognize their existence and to assess their impact on the process of decision making by machine. Such an assessment reveals an essential distinction between decision making in mathematical games as compared with that in the business environment. Decisions made in the course of playing games like chess or contract bridge are unaffected by these human frailties, as are decisions in almost all well-defined mathematical or logical problems. It is in the introduction of the computer into our everyday way of life that the impact of these human qualities is truly felt. Thus the field which is often called "business data processing" emerges as one involving skills quite different from those involved in other better-defined computer fields wherein computers have been, can be, and will be extensively applied. The data processing expert must know the essence of business decisions as well as that of computer programming, he must understand the attitudes of the manager and the person managed, and he must have the experience to reconcile the determination of policy by that management with the implementation of it by machine.

Most computer "experts" have been cautious in discussing their optimistic visions of the future. They are acutely aware that the use of digital computers in business is still in its infancy and consequently that a great many recent case histories demonstrating that the machines have fallen short of expectations can be cited. They are further aware that, to achieve the real benefits that await us from these machines, it will be necessary to uproot organizational relationships and responsibilities which have been developed over many decades and even centuries. Perhaps, in addition to revising the duties of the ranks of clerks who were originally thought to be the only potential "victims" of this "white-collar revolution," a significant effect will also be evident in some echelons of middle management. People will be forced to deal with a device which they do not truly understand and the functions of which are wholly beyond the scope of their training and experience. The prospect of being relegated to a cog in a highly mechanized system, even if it is a cog empowered to make very difficult key decisions, has proved a frightening prospect for the executive whose present role is to supervise a team of people in the performance of the proved functions they and their predecessors have been performing for years.

The manager in this newly automated computer-infested environment must face still another major problem. He must agree in advance on the decisions he would make in a great variety of circumstances as a function of the decisions made by his counterpart in every affected department in the company. It develops that this sort of advance commitment of himself to a decision in a situation wherein he will not be given the opportunity to review his decision in the light of the decisions of other departments of his firm is very difficult for a manager to make. This is true even though he is informed of their decisions at the time they are made and whenever they are changed. Our habits are such that it is disturbing not to have the opportunity to reconsider each decision personally at the time it is made, even though we do not do so and, in fact, did not really have the *capability* to do so in our earlier unmechanized way of doing things.

This strong reluctance to change may indirectly provide us with the explanation for an unexpected development which has taken place as new computer systems are installed. These new systems were billed initially as great savers of personnel in terms of the jobs they were "taking over." But as the machines were installed, it developed that a significant percentage of each of these jobs involved the performance of eminently human functions such as letter writing, telephone answering, and so forth (at least until the entire system was redesigned to eliminate the need for some of these functions). Nevertheless, although the computers failed to "take over" the jobs represented by the functions, they performed as advertised. Postinstallation experience, in those cases where expansions in work load would have required doubling or tripling of the work force before computers were installed, did not actually involve any personnel increase and represented a negligible increase in the work load of the computer.

A further resistance to change is exemplified by the middle manager who wants to make his decisions based on the same reports in the computer system as he has always received before the computer was installed. He expresses his requirements by grandly stating that he believes this expensive computer should provide him with "at least" the same information he had in the precomputer era, and at least as rapidly. Such an attitude, inadequately taking account of its resultant effect, gain or loss, on the new system for data processing which the computer has made possible, represents one of the major factors acting to delay the widespread achievement of benefits from the use of digital computer systems in business organizations.

The responsibility of top management, whose interests

and authority extend over all the functions and objectives of the firm, to select a suitable set of constraints within which the system redesign must take place and then to support the indicated revision of procedures within these constraints must be exercised if we are ultimately to realize the potential of digital computers. The increasing magnitude of this problem is suggested by the transition of the General Motors Corporation from its early character as a corporation whose operating decisions could be made by a small group of men to its present status as a corporation of over one-half million stockholders. In the original form, each manager was completely familiar with the situation about which he was asked to decide. In the present form, no organized group of managers is more than slightly familiar with the meaning of decisions which must be made. At least as far as the data processing machine in a business environment is concerned, the industrialist who was the absolute monarch of all his business surveyed has been replaced by the management "team" which must be managed.

It seems clear that confidence—derived from considerable amounts of successful experience—is the only way in which the practical businessman can, will, and indeed should be convinced that digital computers can be used for decision making in business. With this experience will come an attitude of trust of one's decision-making counterpart in another department in the firm so that operation without continuous human surveillance will become possible. With this experience too will come confidence in automatic decision making.

The requirement for this apprentice period is as it should be. Computers are no better than "anyone else," and it does not seem fair that new computer-based data processing systems should gain acceptance more easily than those old systems for data processing in which decisions were made exclusively by human decision makers.

Furthermore, it is not entirely impossible that presently unforeseen factors (probably human) will limit the operational employment of automatic decision making to an extent far greater than its advocates now believe. This possibility, small though it may be, must be completely eliminated before large business operations can safely be entrusted to decision making devices, however vast their theoretical promise may be.

CHAPTER 6

Hardware Horizons

IN THE PRESENT chapter, we shall attempt to describe data processing hardware of the future. This is done, at least in part, by examining research currently in progress and extrapolating from it. It seems unavoidable, however, for our predictions about what *will* be available in the future to be colored by our ideas of the hardware we would *want* for the future if we could have our choice. The reader should therefore take due account of such predilections and prejudices as are revealed elsewhere in this book. Having done so, he will be in a position to interpret our predictions in their truest light.

Tending further to cloud our crystal ball is the fact that the development of hardware for future application depends largely on the points at which current development funds and other resources are applied by the developing firms. Not without some logical reason, development firms tend to apply these resources where they think they can make the most money rather than where they estimate the best chance is for success of an engineering project.[1] Thus the hardware

[1] A complete discussion of the role actually played by the manufacturer here, along with some ideas on a role which would perhaps benefit everyone more, will be found in Chapter 7, The Role of the Manufacturer.

of the future depends in part on an estimate by the computer manufacturer of what is wanted for the future, and hence of the future market.

Having now made these qualifications, we shall proceed to predict the future data processing hardware of our future business environment.

Engineering developments

Certain major trends in computer engineering developments are already apparent in today's laboratories. These include large decreases in size and electrical power requirements of computers and vast increases in component speed and information capacity. Their impact is likely to reach every component in the computer system. But let us discuss them generally first.

It has been said that the ideal computer of the future will be infinitesimally small and require no external power at all. While our predictions are not intended to extend as far into the future as this, the computers of our conjectures nevertheless represent some significant departures from the computers we know today. We shall discuss these departures in terms of size, power requirements, speed, storage capacity, and reliability. Although these five major kinds of characteristics are highly interdependent, our discussion shall be of each as a separate entity.

Size. Easily observable today is the trend toward miniaturization in electronic components. Television and radio receivers as well as electronic computers have progressed from the vacuum tube 2 or 3 inches in height to the miniature vacuum tube 1½ inches high to the subminiature tube less than 1 inch in height to the subsubminiature tube, etc.

Vacuum tubes, however, are fragile, short-lived, and unstable. In search of something better, engineers have substituted solid-state devices, including such items as the now widely used diode and transistor. These devices, as elements of electronic circuits, differ from electron tubes in several ways, including increased ruggedness and stability, not the least important of which is size. Accomplishing a job equivalent to that of the original 3-inch tube in the electronic circuit, a diode is a thin cylinder only ¼ inch long, and the transistor rectangular and only slightly larger.

But even these substantial reductions in size are modest as compared with what we can expect in the future. It now seems probable that soon entire circuits, each corresponding to one formerly requiring two or three dozen tubes plus the wires necessary to connect them, will be fabricated as single units about the size of a nickel or a dime. In the more distant future, far greater "component" density than that may be achieved. Thus the circuit, rather than the tube or the resistor, will become the basic element for design, and the size of electronic computers will be (further) drastically reduced. Even today, computers the size of an ordinary office desk have been built having far greater capabilities than computers requiring several thousand square feet of floor space only a few years ago.

Power Requirements. Reduction in the power required to operate an electronic computer is important for several reasons. Of these, perhaps the least important is the cost savings involved in terms of the original cost of the installation or of the operating cost. Nevertheless, significant cost savings will derive from the substantial decrease in power requirements which can be expected to result from the trend toward miniaturization. Large-scale computers selling for $1 million or more and *which can operate on ordinary house currents* are now on the market. Decreased power requirements, implying a decrease in the size of the power-supply portion of the computer and hence a further decrease in the size of the computer as a whole, should result in markedly less expensive equipment.

Probably the most significant advantages which can be expected to derive from reductions in power requirements for digital computers are engineering simplicity (and hence greater reliability and maintainability) and computer speed. Simplicity comes about because, as less power must be handled by the circuits employed, fewer circuits are required to do the job. Increased speed of operation comes about because operation is easier and quicker in electronic circuits with lower electron power, just as it is easier and quicker to change the direction of the water from a bathroom faucet than that of the water from a city fire hydrant.

Power reductions down to very low levels present a very strange phenomenon. As the physical size of the device is reduced, the amount of power required to operate it is also reduced. At the same time the circuits and the individual elements of each circuit are brought closer and closer together. Thus these units, capable of operating on extremely low power, are liable to be energized by power intended to energize adjacent units, or even by power external to the computer and not intended for this purpose at all.

Engineering of low-power electronic circuits has developed so far that it has now become necessary to consider fundamental natural limitations. It is not difficult for us to predict, then, that the lower limits in both the size and power of computer circuits ultimately will be determined by these natural limits.

Speed. Whereas early electronic computers required 40 or 50 milliseconds (40/1,000 of a second) to add two numbers, modern computers exist which can accomplish the same thing in a single microsecond (one-millionth of a second) or less. Future computers may be 1,000 times faster than that. Although the vast majority of existing computers are most certainly not in this microsecond class, these superfast computers and faster and faster extensions of them are essential to the solution of presently known problems in the fields of physics and chemistry. By the time we are successful in building the fastest computer of which we can dream today, surely we shall have developed problems requiring computers 1,000 times faster than that in these fields, and perhaps in the field of business management as well.

It is interesting to note that, in some of the electronic circuits presently subject to research in our computer laboratories, limitations imposed by the speed of light actually represent a problem to the engineers. Since light, i.e., electrons, travels at the rate of about 1 foot in 1 milli-microsecond (one-thousandth of a microsecond), addition of numbers at rates approaching this implies the movement of the electrons representing these numbers at a similar rate.

Increases in over-all speed, however, are not derived solely from faster operation of the central computer. In a great many cases the speed of problem solution depends entirely on the speed of input and output. This is especially so in business-type problems. Fortunately, faster means of input, of output, and of internal storage and retrieval of information are also in the offing. Each of these will be discussed in some detail on the following pages.

Capacity for Storage of Information. Early electronic computers could store internally and gain access automatically to only very small amounts of information, represented by forty or fifty numbers. Today many computers each employ several kinds of information storage, different in terms of both speed and capacity. The total information capacity of each such computer may be in excess of 50 million numbers and is as a practical matter unlimited if such nonpermanently accessible media as magnetic tapes are included. Computers of the future will certainly provide us with automatic access to a virtually unlimited store of information.

It is likely that the key to the increase in computer information capacity which has already been realized is the emergence of the art of magnetics as a means for recording information. Magnetic cores, magnetic drums, magnetic disks, magnetic cards, and magnetic tapes are or could be employed today in almost every large-scale computer. Only a very few years ago these techniques were unknown, or at least unemployed, in electronic computer systems.

Even so, the development of information storage capacity is very likely only in its infancy. Magnetic cores so small that 200 to 300 decimal numbers could be stored in the space occupied by an ordinary sewing thimble have been developed. Magnetic tape capable of storing up to 900 numbers on a single square inch of tape is presently in use, and the storage of ten times that much information is presently contemplated. Finally, extremely miniaturized storage devices capable of self organization of the information they contain—so necessary for indexing large random access storage—are now promising to emerge from the laboratories.

Reliability. The final major type of general engineering development we can expect to see in the future is that of vastly improved reliability in components, circuits, equipments, and consequently in the total system. For the most part, the technology has already progressed from electro-mechanical components such as relays into the field of the much more reliable solid-state magnetic devices. From here we can expect to progress to improved solid-state devices manufactured by better methods and thence to newer and still more highly reliable components for digital computers.

Some experience with completely "transistorized" computer devices has now been accumulated. One such device experienced its first transistor failure after a period equivalent to the continuous error-free operation of a single transistor since the birth of Christ. Testing devices of this same general type have proved qualitatively quite satisfying but quantitatively unsatisfying. The number of failures (if any) experienced in a test period of any reasonable length is so low that the statistical significance of the sample does not provide a meaningful error rate.

Startling as has been the increase of 10,000 to 1 in the

reliability of electronic computer components over human operators which we have already experienced, it is likely that another increase of at least equal size is in the offing as the components mentioned above are developed, tested, installed, and utilized in digital computer circuits. Although not all the total computer system can be constructed in this fashion in the foreseeable future, those portions of the system which can be so constructed are in fact presently the least reliable portions, and the improvement in the total system is therefore maximized.

In addition to the kinds of reliability advances mentioned above, the use of such untapped sciences as optics, chemistry, and extremely low temperature magnetics offers further promise, mostly in terms of system components other than those in which reliability has already been substantially improved. Since these techniques are indeed still untried, no pronouncements as to the improvement in reliability which can be expected can be made. In view of the fact that, in general, they will be used in the portions of the system which have remained relatively unreliable, there seems every reason to be optimistic.

Future equipment concepts

At least one-half dozen major computer manufacturers and many more smaller firms are presently working on the problem of developing more efficient and useful computer equipments. Let us discuss some of the directions which this research may take.

Magnetic Tape. Magnetic tape is presently and is likely to remain for some time the primary medium for mass storage of information in digital computer systems. There are, however, several ways in which it can be or is being substantially improved.

Magnetic tape recording of digital information presently represents a relatively weak link in the over-all reliability of the total system. But able people are at work on this problem and it now seems likely that almost error-free tape —perhaps with an impregnable plastic coating affixed— will be developed. With more experience in the mechanical problem of rapidly moving the tape past a magnetic "reading head" capable of detecting the magnetic information recorded on the tape, we gain a sound basis for improvements in the speed and reliability of this operation. And finally the magnetic head itself and its associated circuitry are destined to be improved so that they can discriminate rapidly very densely packed information. This facility, combined with an increase in the number of points at which the information recorded on the tape can be retrieved, will greatly augment the usefulness of magnetic tape in performing its primary function of information storage by augmenting its ability for ready access to that information.

Information rates up to 90,000 alphabetic characters per second have already been achieved. It is likely that magnetic tape devices operating at least ten times that fast will be available in the next generation of computers. These improvements in speed will probably be achieved primarily by increasing the density with which information is packed on the tape—both laterally and longitudinally—and the response of the discrimination circuits, rather than by actually increasing the linear speed of the tape.

But not all improvements in magnetic tape speed are in terms of increases. Important requirements for both very slow and for multispeed tapes have recently been identified. Slow-speed magnetic tapes are required to match the speed of human-operated key-driven devices or of very slow (and presumably inexpensive) computers. Both slow-speed tapes and tapes with a multispeed capability in the low ranges are required to act as the information input and output devices for machines on the order of those presently utilizing punched cards for that purpose. And finally, multispeed tape devices are required to maximize the compatibility between machines with different input or output rates and at the same time minimize the need specially to develop input and output devices for each.

Still another direction which development in the field of magnetic tapes is likely to take is that of incremental tape-drive devices. With such a device, the computer will be able to read or write as much information as it desires—from one alphabetic character to some very large amount of information—on the basis of a single impulse to the tape drive. In this way, it may be possible to eliminate entirely—or at least reduce substantially—the complexity and information capacity of the buffer between the computer and its magnetic tape. Such a development will represent a major improvement in system design.

Information Storage. The capacity of a computer system to store information is really divided into three categories: internal storage, external permanently accessible storage, and external temporarily accessible storage. Of these, only the external permanently accessible storage is not in widespread use at the present time. But let us discuss each of them in turn.

Internal storage capacity in a digital computer has progressed in the past 10 years from only a very few numbers for an entire system to as many as several hundred thousand digits of information per system. Magnetic cores or magnetic drums are not uncommonly used for this purpose, and combinations of both are far from rare. Machines already announced offer more than one million digits of internally stored information, organized in modular units rather than in the single unit common today.

Permanently accessible external storage, as compared with internal storage, usually involves a degradation in the *speed* at which the information stored therein can be retrieved. This is done in order to achieve much greater information *capacity*. This compromise between speed and capacity is common throughout the system but is especially significant here. Since this type of storage is permanently accessible to the central computer, it is sometimes not economical to utilize it for the purpose of retaining historical information. Nevertheless, it is most useful for storing information (such as inventory records) which may rapidly be required at infrequent and unpredictable times. Magnetic disks have achieved some favor for this purpose although they are relatively expensive as a means of storage. The trend that can be discerned is that of decreasingly expensive nonmechanical storage devices, such as magnetic cores or other magnetic devices. As this trend increases, the present distinction between internal and permanent external storage tends to decrease. The ultimate course of this trend seems to be that the distinction will finally disappear between this type of external store and internal computer storage. The several classes of permanent storage which will result will be available each in essentially any capacity at the option of the user, and each in turn will serve the computer according to the dictates of each user in the most efficient way, thus providing an effective balance between speed and capacity in permanently accessible information storage.

Notwithstanding the improvements which are in sight as described above, temporarily accessible external storage is sure to be with us for the foreseeable future. This information is stored temporarily in the system in the sense that the actual medium used for information storage (usually a medium for recording information magnetically or on film) is separate and removable from the mechanism utilized to make the information stored available to the computer. The medium involved may be reels of magnetic tape each more than ½ mile long, strips of tape each less than 1 foot long, or discrete magnetic cards each only a few square inches in area. Information storage on these magnetic media is very inexpensive as compared with permanently accessible external storage media. But the handling and/or reading mechanism may be far from inexpensive in most cases. For this reason, the solution to the problem of storing large quantities of information is usually to provide relatively few handling and reading mechanisms while providing as many discrete pieces of recording media as are necessary to store the information desired.

Applications exist which require active files of one hundred *billion* alphabetic or numeric characters of information. The social security files are an example of such a problem. At the present time, several thousand 10-inch reels of magnetic tapes are required for such storage. Future techniques promise to reduce the space required by a factor of 100 or more, equivalent to storing the text of this book in a single cubic inch.

Some of these applications require that information be retained indefinitely so that it will constitute a historical record with which one could (theoretically) trace each record back to the original transaction which established it. It seems highly probable that files characterized by predictable and orderly access and large quantities of historical information will be retained in computer systems on such media as reels or strips of tape, or cards, recorded magnetically or on film, as far into the future as it is possible to peer.

The Order Repertoire. Since the first electronic computer was announced, nothing significant and indeed almost nothing at all has been done to improve the basic set of orders which the machine can directly understand. However, utilizing the unsophisticated order repertoires which have been provided, computer systems have been programmed and are being programmed to develop their own set of orders from stylized English, mathematical, or other computer languages. The urgency of the requirement to do this increases very rapidly as the complexity and sophistication of computer systems increase.

To date, all the significant advances in this area have been made by—or at least at the behest of—the computer programmers rather than the computer engineers. This has been good from the point of view that the programmers have been more familiar with what *should* be done than the engineers, but it has been bad in that they are in general much less familiar with what *can* be done.

The problem now is to achieve a meeting of the minds of the programmers and the engineers so that we can build computers having the capability to understand instructions quite like those which we would give to the person whose place the computer has managed to usurp. Although such computers are not now in the laboratories or even in the design stage, it seems probable that they are forthcoming by 1970 or 1975. Research in this area is presently being carried out in two or three laboratories across the country. On the success of this and other similar research to be undertaken depends the conquest of one of the most important barriers to the advance of digital computer systems in the business environment of today.

New Devices. Supplementing the improvements mentioned above are certain devices which are pieces of equipment essentially new to digital computer systems. It is sometimes difficult to determine whether these devices are really new or whether they are simply improved versions of existing devices; let us discuss some current and potential developments without bothering to resolve this point.

The automatic reading of a specially printed page is an operation which has already been successfully accomplished in the laboratories and, to a very limited extent, in the field. Numbers printed in magnetic ink on bank checks have been so read, and considerable progress has been made in the development of optical reading of ordinary (nonmagnetic) typewritten or printed information. Once the information has been sensed by either magnetic or optical means, the job of translating that which is sensed into a form suitable for intelligent interpretation by people or machines is a problem in logic (information theory) which is identical in each case. One method for reading such information is to superimpose a grid over each discrete character of information and then to note on a yes or no basis the information content of each square of the grid. The proper balance between grid size, reading speed, and accuracy is the nub of a problem which is well on the way to solution. Automatic recognition of printed data, so long the dream of the science fictionist, now seems assured of attaining reality in the next few years.

In certain somewhat limited cases it will also be possible for handwritten information to be read automatically. Again, this has already been accomplished in the laboratories for fourteen different handwritten and only slightly stylized numbers and symbols. While it is not likely that equipment capable of automatic reading of handwritten information other than that written especially for the automatic reading will be developed, new information, properly styled and entered onto forms developed especially for the purpose, will be entered into computer systems by the most basic of information-recording activities: just writing it down.

The development of magnetic cards and associated devices and methods to handle them rapidly and efficiently seems different enough to be classified as new. Magnetic cards can be characterized as discrete items, on the surface of which information can be recorded and then read. The discrete quality is similar to that of the familiar punched card, while the recording and reading is accomplished much as information is recorded on and read from magnetic tape. Among different concepts under development, size varies from small cards only a few inches across to larger units the size of an ordinary sheet of typewriter paper. The advantages of the magnetic card include automatic reading of information stored thereon, dense packing of information (presently two or three times that of typewritten information and probably ten times that much in the future), a reusable medium of information storage (eliminating the need to retype or repunch entire records to make a single change therein), and in some cases the opportunity automatically and efficiently to handle many cards constituting very large amounts of information.

So-called "high-speed" printers have been highly and widely touted as adjuncts to modern computer systems. Most printers which are classified as "high-speed" print at the rate of from 500 to 1,200 lines per minute (or up to 100 times as fast as a very good typist), equivalent to from sixty thousand to one-quarter million characters a minute maximum rate. Specialized printers operating at about 5,000 lines per minute are available for use in certain applications such as magazine address-label printing.

But in reality these numbers have very little meaning in themselves. A printing device is truly high-speed only with respect to the application to which it is put. It is necessary to answer such questions as: How accurately can we expect the device to print? Can we expect the printer to be in working order and available for a job when there is printing to be done? Can the printer produce reproducible copy? Can it make several carbons? Will specialized printing loads such as single-letter printing or the use of only the right-hand ten columns place an undue strain on the mechanism? and so forth, ad infinitum.

Applications which have any built-in requirement for printer speeds in excess of those readily available today are very rare indeed. As the art of data processing gains in sophistication and status over the years, the trend will be to produce more and more condensed summaries of information in place of lengthy reports so that the resulting printing load will be further reduced. But the continued existence of applications requiring communication with each individual magazine subscriber, each savings bond holder, or each member of the Federal old age pension program will provide the need in a few specialized cases such as these for faster and faster printers in the years to come.

Mechanical printers are probably limited in usable speed to about 1,000 to 1,500 lines of printing per minute. But the development of printing techniques utilizing electro-static, chemical, and magnetic processes provides the means to push the upper limit in speed far beyond these figures. These techniques, possibly combined with photographic recording mechanisms, probably will enable us to produce printed copy at the prodigious rate of 10,000 lines per minute or more if we so desire. Let us hope that the use of these very high printing speeds is confined to those applications which exhibit a fundamental requirement for it and that they are not permitted to sully an otherwise well-thought-out process of scientific control and management of a business firm.

The final area of equipment advance we wish to mention here is somewhat more "off the beaten track" than those mentioned above and is furthermore considerably farther from successful completion. We refer here to the operation of automatic recognition of audible speech. Although at the present time there are not any successful (in the sense of being useful) examples of equipment in action with the capability automatically to recognize audible speech, several laboratories are working in this area. Controlled experiments have resulted in the successful automatic recognition of spoken sounds with 98 per cent accuracy from among a small set of possible sounds presented to the machine. New approaches which separate the engineering problem of individual sound recording from the logical or probabilistic one of recognition and discrimination of the recorded sounds appear to be quite promising.

Potential applications of such a device range from voice-operated typewriters and grocery store check-out devices to full-scale digital computer systems capable of being controlled directly by spoken commands. One of the most interesting and perhaps useful such possible applications is that to machine translation of a *spoken* language into another language, spoken or printed. No doubt all sorts of other interesting possibilities suggest themselves to the reader.

In the case of this type of device, however, the conceptual and engineering problems involved are so great and so far removed from the present state of our knowledge that

many years are likely to pass before any application can be
achieved. Furthermore, applications of the scope and complexity of some of those mentioned above probably will
require several decades to achieve their complete development and implementation. It is nevertheless heartening to
know that research is under way in connection with ideas of
such a fundamental nature as this one.

Design and construction of computer systems of the future

When one considers how new the art of digital computer
application to any problem really is (especially the application to business data processing problems), one is probably
amazed that these applications have gone as far and have
been accepted as well as they have. It is to be confidently
anticipated that the future will reveal advances of this kind
at an even more rapid rate than the past. Several improvements which impinge on the over-all system are available in
the present hardware; let us discuss a few that come to mind.

Organization of Information. Perhaps the area in which
broad improvements are most obviously needed is that of
the organization of information to which the computer
system has either automatic access or access with the aid
of human intervention. Really large files of information
containing several million records have not yet been
mechanized in a satisfactory fashion. The problem of extracting data from the world of reality into the computer
system (called the "input" problem) has not really been
solved. Nor do the ultimate solutions to these problems
appear to be just around the corner. Nevertheless, we are
firmly convinced that the problem of establishing a rapport

between the clerical, mathematical, or logical activity of processing, and the handling of the data which have been and are to be processed will be satisfactorily resolved by 1970.

This apparent optimism is not entirely without foundation. Already mentioned have been devices which will read printed copy, feed information rapidly into a computer, or speedily print the output so as to make it intelligible to the human operators. In the area of very large files we have cited our findings that very large random access files and extremely fast sequential access files are imminently upon us. Additional examples of work in this field include a cooperative program to standardize information recording on magnetic tape so that the tapes can be transferred from one machine to any other as dictated by the desired flow of information. This same problem has also been approached from the standpoint of building devices capable of automatic translation from one type of magnetic tape information used by (one machine of) one computer manufacturer to those of another. The problem of very large files has been attacked from the standpoint of logical file organization, including the coding and placement of information so that it can be more readily located and retrieved. Some progress has even been made toward a device which has the capability to retrieve from a file a record identified by a particular piece of coding without explicit identification, either by mechanized or human elements external to the device or by the device itself, of the location of that record in the file.

The whole field of information retrieval has been so

recently recognized as a useful field of research that little progress has been revealed to date. But the very fact that this field is now receiving the attention—and, more importantly, the technical and financial support—of several important private and government agencies is sufficient reason to believe that important logical and technological break-throughs are imminent.

Systematic Design of Optimum Computer Configurations. It has been said that no fundamental improvements in the design of digital computers have been developed since the method of designing them was first specified by John von Neumann at Princeton University in 1946. While we do not believe this statement to be entirely true, we do concede that there is considerable room for improvement. Fortunately, again, this improvement seems about to come to pass.

Let us make clear to begin with that there are really at least four levels of computer design: component design (e.g., transistors and diodes), circuit design (e.g., circuits to add together two decimal numbers), equipment design (e.g., punched card reading devices and magnetic core information buffers), and system design (e.g., the optimum configuration of equipment most effectively to solve the problems at hand). Methods of design at these different design levels are likely to be advanced in widely different ways.

Component design techniques have been augmented by the use of digital computers for the numerical solution of problems in solid-state physics, and hence relating to basic aspects of computer component theory. But indeed most of the advances here, substantial as they are, are the results of improvements in physical theory based on empirical results related thereto.

Rather recently, *circuit design* has been carried out almost entirely automatically by employing digital computers to process the logical equations which define the equipment and to produce the optimum configuration of components to achieve this result. This technique is already very popular and it is likely that within a very few years efficient design of complex pieces of digital computer equipment will dictate the use of a digital computer in this fashion whenever a new computer is designed.[2]

We have discussed *equipment design* at some length in this chapter. In the past 10 years, we have seen input and output speeds increased a hundredfold, internal computing speeds increased many thousandfold, and the capacity to store information internally increased almost to a point of diminishing returns. But none of these advances seems to be the result of improved equipment design *techniques*. They have been achieved largely by making use of better components, and in most cases by progressing from mechanical to electron tube to solid-state electronic or magnetic components. It will now be necessary to develop equipment design techniques much like the component

---

[2] Closely related to this technique is that employed currently by a large electrical manufacturing firm. By the use of a digital computer, this firm is able to develop the detailed design of standard types of electric motors directly from the customer's specifications which are fed directly to the machine. The decreases in design cost and the speedier customer service thereby gained have served to generate a substantial interest in this type of computer application.

design techniques described previously, and so to develop the capability economically to tailor equipment to particular applications in which it is employed.

In spite of all the above improvements in design techniques which we have experienced, the problem of *system design* remains the key to any real advancement in the hardware for the business data processing technology. Given that money and talent can be directed toward designing and building a computer system which computes faster, stores more information in the internal storage, has faster access to that information, or can accept input data more rapidly from its input devices, the questions arise as to which of these things should be emphasized and what is the proper balance among them (and, of course, among many more possibilities which have not been mentioned in this illustration).

This is essentially the problem of system design, i.e., the determination of the equipment complement most suitable to solve the problem. To date, no satisfactory techniques have been found for answering these questions. We are entirely without any systematic (and certainly without any analytic) approach to the solution. Although several agencies are now tackling this problem on their own or under government sponsorship, it seems highly improbable that any satisfactory general solution will be found before the next generation of computers is upon us; and in fact it seems unlikely that one will be found before the next several generations have passed.

There is, however, a growing intuitive grasp, based solely on the actual experience gained to date, in the field of computer system design and selection for a particular problem. This "intuition" will stand us in good stead (whenever those with problems of this type avail themselves of it); moreover, it will provide an ever-broadening base on which we must build any successful systematic solution to the problem. An "expert," after all, is simply a man whose experience and good sense enable him to make "good" decisions when he is in possession of only some of the relevant facts.

Total Design. By way of illustrating the problem of total design of a computer system—the problem which impinges on all levels of design from component design to system design—we wish to mention a very gross trend which can be observed.

To an ever-increasing extent, computer systems are tending to be composed of smaller basic components, each using less power and doing less work, and to be composed of these components in far greater numbers than were their computer ancestors. Obviously, then, the problem of the total organization of the system is increased tremendously by the fact that the designer now finds himself with more and more basic units with which he must accomplish a job.

It has been estimated [3] that the number of nerve cells in the average adult human brain is about 10^{10}, the reaction speed of a single neuron is on the order of about one thousand per second, and the size of these neurons is such that about 10 million of them can be packed in a single cubic

[3] John von Neumann, *Computer and the Brain*, Yale University Press, New Haven, Connecticut, 1958.

centimeter. These figures illustrate the fact that the human brain is characterized by a very large number of very small elements, each operating rather slowly as compared with a modern computer element, and all working together to produce a very complex operation.

Presently known computers, theoretically involving as many as 10^8 elements, each capable of over a million reactions per second, are in a sense not vastly different from this brain. Only with regard to size is the discrepancy between the artificial device and the natural automata striking. There are on the order of 100 times more elements in the brain than in this computer, and each brain element is perhaps 100,000 times smaller than its computer counterpart. But the advantage of the artificial device by a factor of 1,000 in speed tends somewhat to balance these deficiencies out. This balance has noticeably improved over the short life of the digital computer and can be expected to improve further as our abilities in this area increase.

Scientists have not yet been able to determine the precise physical organization of the cells of the human brain. Perhaps when they do they will derive some clue as to the optimum organization of the growing number of smaller and smaller computer components which comprise each successive generation of digital computer systems.

Pending the solution of this problem of total design by analogy to the organization of the human brain—or by any other means—our difficulties in this area continue to grow. Increase in complexity of computer systems has already resulted in delays of a full year or more in construction, solely as a result of our inability rapidly to organize the numerous components which comprise the circuits of our system.

The removal of this fundamental roadblock to progress is highly desirable; the force behind this removal is regrettably unapparent at this time.

Beyond the horizon

Data processing systems of the future will employ many of the devices mentioned on the previous pages. It will be necessary to develop techniques for utilizing these devices which in some cases will be entirely different from those in use today. The task of identifying and developing the devices and related techniques which will most favorably achieve the objectives of the business organization will remain for decades to come the fundamental barrier to the true automation of business data processing.

Although we cannot hope, therefore, to specify on these pages the kind of system which *should* exist in 1980, we propose alternatively to describe a fictional system which *might* exist. By describing here an automated data processing system for a large manufacturing company of the future, we hope to illustrate not only the direction which equipment and system development is taking but to give some idea of the nature and importance of the increasing interaction between man and the machines which serve him.

General Satellites, a Manufacturing Firm. Each employee of General Satellites (GS) will carry a card which identifies him. The card will carry such information as his name and employee number in a form readable by both machines and people, while other information such as salary rate and security clearance will be carried in an invisible machine-coded form. As each employee arrives in the morning, works on one job and then another, and leaves at night, his card is inserted into and read by an automatic reading device which records these facts and transmits them to the Processing Unit (PU) of the company.

Production schedules and achievements are also monitored by the PU, together with an exact count of the inventory available at each point for production and a tally of the number of products produced. As the inventory falls below the amount required for production, the appropriate action is signaled to the supervisor by the PU. And as the required number of items emerges from the production line, the PU will have already signaled the beginning of production of the next product.

Far-off sales will be programmed automatically to affect the activities of production. If actual GS sales fall below the expected sales (with which reported sales are compared periodically), production is slowed. If sales of GS products exceed expectations, item production is automatically increased. If actual sales differ alarmingly from the predicted norms, top management is notified so that corrective action can be taken for this or other lagging products.

Payroll production is readily available from the information already entered into the data processing system. But information which may be of more immediate importance to management is also readily obtainable. If a man who supervises a key station on the production line is absent, the production schedule is automatically altered accordingly and alternate personnel notified. If a message is received from a potential customer requesting an item not regularly produced, its price is automatically determined by the PU on the basis of up-to-date costs of production, some preference given to regular customers (if such is the policy of GS), the customer notified, and the order consummated.

Top management is interested in trends. These are indicated, over both the long and short term, graphically in the president's office. Unusual departures are highlighted, and local and industry-wide files are consulted from among the vast store of information available. It will fall then to management to make major policy decisions which maximize the effectiveness of the capital invested. By instructing the PU to solve a set of equations representing mathematically the objectives of the firm, management will test alternative decisions theoretically without incurring the costs associated with their actual implementation.

What has become of the people in this automated manufacturing firm—the clerks and the workers on the line? Most are enjoying their vastly increased leisure, at any given time. Others are still GS employees in interesting important jobs. And still others are employed by firms making some of the many new products which our new society demands. The history of machines has been to create jobs to offset the ones they eliminate, and generally to improve our standard of living. It seems clear that, over the long run, automation in business data processing will have a similar effect.

Perspective of Systems Design. To achieve a data processing system resembling that of General Satellites, it will be necessary to improve substantially both equipment and our techniques for using this equipment. Evidence of progress in both objectives is increasingly noticeable.

It remains, however, for automatic data processing systems to gain the confidence and enthusiasm of the people whom they must serve. This confidence, gained from a familiarity and understanding of the activities and devices involved, is essential to success. It will result only from careful planning and implementation, but dynamic and courageous action will be required of the system pioneers. Scientific management—made possible by modern data processing equipment and techniques—seems now to represent our next industrial frontier.

CHAPTER 7

The Role of the Manufacturer

HAVING ESTABLISHED the fact that the electronic computer industry is a permanent and rapidly growing fixture in our society, it now becomes pertinent to inquire into the role which has been played by the computer manufacturers in this development and into the role which they can be and should be expected to play in the future.

Recent surveys have shown that new products of all kinds represent an ever-increasing percentage of our gross national product. Research expenditures of private industry as a whole nearly doubled in the period from 1953 to 1957 and reached a rate of about $7.3 billion annually in 1958. These expenditures were made in the expectation of future profits as a direct result thereof or, in a few cases, in accordance with some feeling of moral responsibility for product improvement. Very substantial additional expenditures were made of government funds (mostly Federal government), almost entirely in view of the responsibility of government to support such research, but occasionally with some particular essentially competitive project in mind.

This general trend is certainly identifiable in the computer market. As compared with the total dollar value of its product, the computer industry has been the recipient of far more than its share of this research money. It is almost certain that this unbalanced situation will continue for some time to come.

In addition to his activity in the research field, the computer manufacturer plays by far the major role in sales of his product, although he is sometimes aided significantly in this endeavor by universities, research firms, and commercial consulting firms. This implies his extensive participation in computer applications, but to a degree which varies widely with the manufacturer and the customer. Secondly, the computer manufacturer often participates directly in computer application studies and sometimes even in the operation of computer systems installed as a result thereof, again to a degree which varies widely with the manufacturer and the application. And finally, the manufacturer has usually accepted the role of maintaining the equipment he sells or leases, often assuming complete responsibility for this important activity.

Thus in his roles as researcher, salesman and applications engineer, operator, and maintenance man, the computer manufacturer plays a vital part in the digital computer field —a part probably more vital and of broader scope than any other manufacturer plays in connection with his product. Let us examine, then, in some detail, this role as it has been in the past and as we believe it should be in the future.

Objectives and the computer manufacturer

Although plans for the construction of digital computers on a semiproduction basis were first formulated commercially as recently as 3 or 4 years after World War II, the great need for this product and the resulting high demand were such as to produce an environment for product acceptance unlike any this country had ever experienced. A situation in which the demand for a large expensive product was substantially in excess of the supply existed, even though the purpose of such a product (in business applications) was not clearly understood and the techniques for its use were almost unknown.

In some respects it is relevant to reflect upon the automobile industry shortly after the turn of the century, at which time there were about sixteen hundred independent manufacturers of automotive vehicles in the United States, almost all of whose products possessed substantial development potential. Today, only six automobile manufacturers remain. In the interim, a sound basis for the technically and financially successful manufacture of automobiles was found. The elements of this basis proved to be sound financing, high technical competence, competent management, a high degree of flexibility, good forecasting, and some sprinkling of luck.

No such basis for the computer manufacturing industry has yet been found. In the face of an even more complex problem than that which faced the auto industry (involving not only the manufacture but the use of the product), it does not seem likely that such a basis will be found in the near future.

As is the case in most manufacturing industries, the manufacturer and the user of digital computers are to a large extent at cross purposes. The primary objective of the man-

ufacturer is to make money—in the long or the short run—
by selling (or renting) equipment. The user, on the other
hand, wants to make money by using equipment. Thus large
expenditures for research and development of new products
tend to mitigate against the manufacturer's objectives but,
to the extent that they result in a better product, tend to
favor the objectives of the user. Similarly, continued production of proved products whose development costs have
long since been amortized by the manufacturer favors his
objectives while acting in opposition to those of the user.

At any given time in the history of data processing equipment, the extensive use of any particular piece of equipment
or media tends to produce a relatively large amount of
inertia. The very common information storage medium
of eighty-column punched cards is a case in point. These
cards, on which up to eighty alphabetic or numeric characters can be represented by punching holes in a particular
format, are still very much in the data processing picture
in substantially the same form as 40 years ago. During
this period, and especially within the last half dozen years,
many preferable designs have been proposed and a few even
tested and implemented. Yet the facts that so much information is now recorded in punched card form and that so many
machines are now in use which are able to "read" this information seem to dictate their continued existence for some
time to come.

Not every aspect of this inertia is bad, from the standpoint of either the user or the manufacturer. Its alternative
might very well be the development of a great many
products of similar purpose such that a new and more

devastating inertia of incompatibility among them would be created, representing a major impediment to progress in the entire field of data processing. The field of manufacturing data processing equipment is yet young and growing; radical ideas for new products to accomplish the old or the newly identified jobs therefore remain essential to continued progress in the field.

Partly as a result of the newness of the field and partly because of its complexity, substantial disagreement remains among the experts as to the best products on which to freeze. Thus who can say what the optimum format is for information recorded on magnetic tape? Who can say what the optimum type of order code for a computer is, much less the specific orders it should contain? And who can determine the optimum arrangement of processor, internal storage, and external storage, even for a particular class of problems?

It is probably well at this time and for some time to come that arguments on either side of these disagreements continue to be relatively well balanced. As long as this is the case, the computer manufacturing firms will continue to develop new and better devices, and the users will continue to test and evaluate them and to suggest improvements within the highly competitive framework of free enterprise.

As this development proceeds along the way toward eventual standardization of equipment and techniques, we must be constantly on guard against the confusion which tends to arise between standardization and compatibility. It is almost certain that long before we are in a position to construct *standard* items for tasks like reading and storing information and computing, we shall be in a position to offer *compatible* items of equipment for these jobs. Thus information which can be read by one computer can also be read by another, information which is stored in one computer system can be utilized by another, and programs which are written for one computer can be readily adapted to another. Some progress has already been made in some of these areas but we must be constantly alert for new opportunities to increase compatibility between and among existing and newly developed computer systems. Such an effort will result in a substantial reduction in the size of the formidable task of the utilization of digital computer systems.

Finally, it is necessary—in achieving our objectives of major improvements in the data processing art—to avoid the resulting temptation to reject ostensibly small improvements in favor of the major ones which seem to be just around the corner. In addition to the rather obvious reason that improvements which seem to be just around the corner have a habit of not materializing as we expect them to, it is often true that the sum of several "small" improvements in technology results in one or several very major improvements indeed. Thus, while we cannot, in today's technology, achieve very large files of random access storage at a price comparable with serial storage, the introduction of random access storage at a much higher price is likely to result in further technological improvements by virtue of the research, engineering, and manufacturing experience gained and is certain to result in the widespread development of techniques for the utilization of random access storage in digital computer systems.

Research and development

A modern large manufacturer in the computer field can be expected to allocate 10 to 20 per cent of his net profits to research and the development of new devices in the field. In addition to this, an increasingly large amount of Federal government support can be found for projects to develop equipment for which a government need has been defined. Much but not all of this government support is for military purposes. Most of the nonmilitary government projects and some of the military ones—especially in the field of military logistics—result in products which are useful not only toward the purpose for which they were intended but as tools for industrial use throughout the data processing community.

There is, however, a single aspect of research and development in the digital computer field which identifies this effort as strikingly different from the research and development effort undertaken in any other product field: The utilization of the digital computer as an integral part of an operating business firm involves both a highly detailed technical knowledge of all the interactions of the *firm* within the scope of the computer activities, and an advanced skill level in *computer use*. Consider the contrast between this situation and that in the automobile manufacturing industry, for example, where, although it is difficult to *engineer* the product, its proper *use* does not present any difficult problems. Similarly, the engineering *design* of a modern skyscraper is a highly specialized skill, even among engineers, but the use of the building constructed as a result of this design is no problem.

There are, to be sure, examples which may be cited to demonstrate the relatively straightforward use of a computer (but involving techniques vastly more complex than those involved in the use of an automobile or a skyscraper). These examples are now known to represent a very small minority of the class of successful large-scale computer applications in business across the United States; to assume that success in data processing will be achieved at a low level of understanding of computer use (and of the system implemented) represents a risk far larger than most competitive firms can afford to assume.

Because of this importance of product utilization, the potential manufacturer of any large-scale digital computer system is faced with a unique problem in the research and development of his product: While it is he who has developed the capability to accomplish research which will lead to the development of new and useful products, it is not he but his customer, the potential user of this equipment, who is in a position (if, indeed, anyone is) to say what products need to be developed. The very fact that this manufacturer is not primarily a user of his product but its engineer suggests that he lacks the experience in the use of such products necessary to develop the proper ones. Engineers who have developed a particular automotive product know, for example, that it should be driven at certain speeds for most economical operation and longer life. These same engineers are in the best position to know the value of a redesigned braking system to this vehicle, and since any braking system is activated by depressing the brake pedal, techniques for brake utilization are not likely to influence their decision on this point.

In the computer situation, however, the engineer is not in such a fortunate position. Although he can often program the computer, he is inexperienced in the operational use of the devices he designs—e.g., he has not been required daily to maintain a file of 100,000 checking accounts in a commercial bank or to accumulate hourly the data which reflect the work done in a job shop. His engineering skill does not extend into the art of coping with problems revealed only by the real problems of use. The engineering skills involved in the construction of a piano are one thing, while the problem of playing the instrument to produce a given effect is entirely different (and not usually best solved by the design engineer).

Some of the larger manufacturers of computers have attempted to solve this problem by adding so-called "applications specialists" to their staff. This solution suffers from two defects. These people, skilled though they may be when they are added to the staff, tend to become farther and farther removed from the problems of day-to-day computer operation as their association with productive data processing fades into the past, and more interested in the "successful" operation of the equipment itself; for this reason, in most cases their usefulness for this purpose diminishes with time. Secondly, these people are often unable, organizationally or personally, to communicate with the engineers who so badly need the kind of advice these specialists are intended to provide; this situation unnecessarily results in a product inadequately oriented toward any particular use in the world in which it must operate.

We have then a different problem in digital computer research and development—one which has come upon us only with the recent advent of machines with the capability to perform automatically the previously ill-defined data processing operations of any large business organization. Substantial resources are available to do the job, reluctantly at the manufacturers' plant and of necessity in the offices of the customer, present and potential. How then can these very large resources be most usefully employed in research and development of digital computer systems?

Research. Very little engineering capability to develop new products in the data processing field exists today outside the confines of the commercial manufacturing firms in the field. The National Bureau of Standards has developed some equipment for government use which was not otherwise available at the time of its development. Some of this equipment has been quite successful, and commercial firms have followed suit in several cases. Several major universities have done basic research and designed and constructed equipment mostly for their own use. Some of this equipment too has filled a serious void, especially in the early days of automatic digital computing.

But with respect to equipment available for the ordinary industrial user, by far the major role in basic and applied research is left to the data processing manufacturer. It is he who has, in the last analysis, the resources—both dollar and manpower—to perform the research which must be done before new products can be developed in the data processing field.

At the same time that the manufacturer has developed this capability and hence responsibility for research, objectives in direct conflict with these have also been nurtured. These are the profit objectives which have such a major impact on all the activities of every manufacturer in a competitive industry. In the early period of the development of data processing equipment, first any product at all and then fundamental (and hence long-range) improvements in that product represented the major objectives of each firm in the field. The very fact that so few competitors existed reduced the need for the rapid introduction of more and more products onto the market.

Now, however, the situation has changed. While it is obviously still true that any fundamental break-through in the state of the art would place the company fostering this break-through in a very advantageous position, the pressure to meet the fire of his competitors with rapidly set fires of his own is most tempting to any sales organization. To be in a position to do this as often as possible, it becomes necessary sometimes to curtail certain research and development until the competitive market situation provides the greatest advantage for proceeding. Thus the criteria become, to a certain extent, how will the introduction of this product affect our total market position, rather than will the introduction of this product represent an advance in the quality and capability of data processing equipment available to customers.

The case for fundamental research leading to the development of entirely new products is perhaps more complex than we have made it seem. Most small manufacturers are in the position of having to introduce a better product in order to break into or stay in the market at all; most of the larger manufacturers are not. Any manufacturer must take into account the inertia which has been built up and which surrounds the product or system he expects to replace, however good his product may seem to be. And for the sake of continued activity in research, and, in fact, continued existence in the computer manufacturing field, each manufacturer *must* conduct his over-all operation in such a way as to maximize his profits over the short run, if austere financing is involved, and over the long run in every case. It is important to consider this requirement as we attempt to place the manufacturer's activities in proper perspective.

Development and Manufacturing. Successful experience in the techniques of production is of vital importance to successful development and manufacture of data processing equipment. Such experience, obtained either individually by the members of the firm or by the firm itself, is necessary if a fairly priced, adequately reliable, easily maintainable product is to be produced. The numerous exceptions which can be cited do not in our opinion discredit the truth of this rule. It is possible, for example, that a prototype computer can be built which operates in a highly satisfactory way and that at no time subsequently will its manufacturer be in a position to produce successfully production-line copies of this machine on a continuing basis. While the responsibility for solving this problem rests entirely with the manufacturer of the equipment, its potential effect on the user is obvious.

Small, sometimes specialized, manufacturers must approach the production problem rather differently from large generalized organizations. The cost savings that sometimes result from this operating efficiency and singleness of purpose of the small firm are sometimes counterbalanced by the greater technical competence of the larger firm.

The specialized problem of whether to develop special equipment for a given special purpose is similar to the general problem of development vs. manufacturing and occurs surprisingly frequently. It often takes on the following form: Over the several weeks or months of the development stages of the data processing system, as the user's discussion passes from the definition of the problem and centers around the selection of equipment, equipment features which would be desirable but which are not yet commercially available are often identified. Sometimes these features have already been incorporated in equipment which is well past the manufacturer's planning stage; sometimes they represent only very advanced thinking on the part of the manufacturer; and only rarely are they representative of ideas not yet considered by the manufacturer.

In any case where equipment selection extends to devices which are not presently in production or forthcoming imminently, a new problem of system design and implementation has been created. Whenever the choice of additional features is not made exclusively from among equipment in production on the particular target date for equipment acquisition, *all* the vast possibilities of *future* hardware development are brought into the picture. Consequently, since (1) these possibilities cannot be realized on the target date, and (2) the date of the availability of these as yet unproduced features is itself a necessarily inaccurate estimate, consideration of the employment of planned but unproduced equipment exhibiting these features must be separated from that of equipment available on a definite schedule.

This distinction between presently available equipment and systems and those probably available in the future has proved extremely difficult to make. The final responsibility for making it falls to the prospective user. Failure to make it (sometimes as a result of irresponsible claims of production skill made by the manufacturer) has all too frequently contributed to costly delays in the installation of a new data processing system.

Similarly, the potential using organization must also become aware of the very long time involved from the initial decision by the manufacturer to build a new computer, through the design, prototype, test, and manufacturing stages to the availability of a production model. It is not unrealistic to suppose that the time required for this job is in the area of 4 or 5 years for a completely new set of equipment. It is the responsibility of computer manufacturers to make this fact quite clear to their potential customers. It is or should be relevant to the planning of the organization which expects to use the new equipment in several ways: It dictates the extent to which the development of the data processing program should be centered around the present equipment; and consequently it enables one to estimate the form, complexity, and size of the problem to which the new equipment could be applied.

Sales and applications

Efforts of computer manufacturers to advertise their products extend far beyond potential customers to the general readers of popular magazines, newspapers, and to radio listeners and television viewers safely situated and relaxed in their homes. This "institutional" advertising attempts to establish the idea that modern data processing systems can solve the most complex of business problems at reasonable cost and with the greatest of ease of planning and operation and, of course, that the equipment advertised is so superior to that of the competitors that it is really pointless to consider the alternatives.

Indeed, every manufacturer of any advertised product—computer or otherwise—attempts to show the superiority of his equipment over that of his competitors in every possible way. While among such items as automobiles or refrigerators there probably is really very little to choose, such is most certainly not the case with data processing equipment. With respect to every aspect of its manufacture and use, the differences among the data processing equipment of the several manufacturers (and in many cases even that offered by a single manufacturer) could hardly be wider. Its cost, its efficiency, its speed—in general, its suitability for a particular application—are often delicately sensitive to the many characteristics of the problem and to the objectives of management in utilizing the machines.

But unlike most other manufactured products, establishing the "characteristics of the problem" to which a digital system is to be applied is itself a very difficult problem. In a great many cases, the job of describing the data processing problem with sufficient accuracy and detail that a computer can be applied to its solution is far more difficult, time-consuming, and costly than solving the problem with the computer once this description is complete.

It is for this reason that, even though the choice of a

particular computer system often depends on the all-important characteristics of the problem, a system other than that which would provide the best solution—and occasionally one which will not solve the problem at all—is chosen.

Here again, however, the problem solution is not so simple as it seems. Surely the cost of the study to determine the best system to install must be included in the installation cost. Further, one must include the cost of any direct savings which could have been achieved but were delayed because of this study; and it may very well be that one's competitors could gain no advantage if the new system were installed immediately.

But probably the most important reason that we cannot always choose the "best" computer system for the problem is simply that it is impossible to *know* certain characteristics of the problem until the implementation is actually under way. This in turn implies that one must have the benefit of actual operating experience before one can select the best method of operation. Thus a suitable solution is dependent upon the results of previous solutions and the process must at best be a converging one. Since we are faced not only with an ever-growing fund of knowledge about problem solution but, in the business society, with ever-changing problems, our approximation to the best solution is seen to be a highly fleeting matter of experience, knowledge, and judgment.

Neither computer manufacturer nor potential user acts as though this were true. Lengthy "feasibility studies" are carried out by the user, after which invitations to bid are issued to several manufacturers, subject to which several "proposals" are prepared, on the basis of which the proposals are "evaluated" and a selection is made. There is unfortunately often very little significance to all this activity. Such a procedure places the manufacturer in a position where he tends to exaggerate the capability of his product in an effort to make the sale and at the same time provides the user with information which is not sufficiently detailed and tested to be reliable.

Here indeed lies one of the major problems of sales and applications in the computer field: In either the institutional advertising situation or the one in which the bidding for the sale is highly competitive, the manufacturer is likely to portray his product at the (true) upper limit of its capability. The problem arises when, having made his sale on this at least theoretically sound basis, the manufacturer begins to feel overly extended, adopts a very conservative attitude about the actual use of his product (to ensure its "success"), and thus fails to realize the potential benefits for which the equipment was obtained.

As the party with the most experience and knowledge in the field, it is often the manufacturer and not the user (again in contrast with most manufactured products) who faces the responsibility of extending the application of his product into new and uncharted, and potentially more beneficial, fields. The facts that the new and uncharted road is risky and that these risks would accrue to the manufacturer after the product had been sold—and thus jeopardize the success of the application after the period of necessary risks associated with sales had passed—mitigate against his advising the user that the added risks of new applications be assumed.

There are, of course, risks associated with the application of new and untried techniques, involving the use of digital computers, which must be borne by the presumed beneficiary of these applications. The fact that computer applications such as sales analysis, market analysis, job shop production scheduling, and personnel qualification analysis are new suggests that these applications, as initially programmed for the computer, may be erroneous and hence may not reflect the true state of affairs (e.g., the sales or market picture). In such a case, the fear that the solution of these problems on a digital computer system might not be successful is well founded. Although such failures are rarely due to the failure of the computing equipment to operate as advertised, they are nonetheless real. As compared with the more widely known risks of equipment failure, these may result in equally or even more serious difficulties, both financial and procedural, for the using firm.

Occasionally risks of operational success will depend primarily on the success or failure of the computing equipment involved to operate as anticipated. Such risks are usually significant only when the equipment itself is newly developed and hence has not been operationally tested; they are of course greatly compounded by the added burden of a new and untried solution to a knotty and pressing problem.

This difficulty of being at the forefront of either the applications or engineering state of the art will probably be overcome on a broad scale only with time. Advanced applications, which have involved an assumption of a full share of the risk associated with embarking as a pioneer into the promising but untried, are in successful operation today. Some of them are cited in Chapter 9. But the natural reluctance exhibited to date on the part of both the manufacturers and users of digital computing equipment to engage in promising but untried applications—and largely by the manufacturer in the introduction of new equipment—represent a major diversion in the course of progress of digital computer applications. The student, the public, and the potential user must be trained and must gain a certain amount of experience (i.e., proof) before they can and are willing to accept a substantial portion of the benefits which the modern digital computer system seems to offer.

Equipment operation

In most cases of commercial use of computing equipment the actual operation of that equipment—as distinguished from its maintenance—is the responsibility solely of its user. There are, to be sure, a very few cases where outside parties, e.g., consultants, have been retained on contract to carry out the actual operation of the machines, but these represent only a small minority of all applications of digital computer systems.

On the question of programming (specifying the individual steps by which a particular machine is to accomplish the job at hand), the attitude toward manufacturer assistance is quite different. Although a few manufacturers provide very little help in this regard, most manufacturers have found it necessary or desirable to develop very capable programming staffs of their own, solely for the purpose of assisting customers in the design of their computer programs and the consequent operation of the equipment installation.

It is probable that without such help a very large portion of today's computer users would not have been able to operate their installations in a satisfactory (i.e., profitable) fashion. Lacking the knowledge and experience required for such operation, most users would have found themselves without access to the techniques necessary to prevent prolonged delays in achieving successful, meaningful operation, the precursor to retrenchment from the vast potentials of the modern data processor to the manual or electromechanic systems of the past.

By carrying out efforts to develop these operating techniques for their equipment, computer manufacturers have in most cases performed a great service to the industry as a whole. Yet today potential users of the equipment demand, now from another quarter, still more emphasis on computer applications. The emergence of large organizations of users of particular computing equipment to promote better applications practices of that equipment has been the result. As compared with the efforts of the manufacturers, these organizations have by cooperative effort been able to develop more programs for computer operation (as a result of the sheer size of the effort involved), programs more nearly reflecting the operating needs of the users (as a result of the common interests of the organization members or simply their greater familiarity with the operating problems encountered) and, in some cases, machine characteristics which would enhance the efficiency of the product to such an extent that they were able to convince or force the manufacturer to adopt them.

While the activities of these cooperative users' organizations are in no way the responsibility of the computer manufacturer, their existence has increasingly been vital to his interest if indeed it has not become his responsibility. Some potential users have found it advisable to include in a contract with the equipment company a clause which permits the contract to be canceled at the time the equipment is ready to be delivered if no suitable user's organization exists at that time.

Perhaps the primary significance of this cooperative organization, and of the user's and manufacturer's relationship to it, is its implication about the problems of operation: These problems are of such scope and complexity that the combined efforts of the manufacturer, the user, and his colleagues and competitors are required for successful operation. Throughout the industrial revolution, no other manufactured product has required this extensive concentration of procedural know-how to achieve its successful introduction into the contemporary commercial environment. When employed so as to realize the maximum possible portion of their potential advantage, digital computers represent a sharp upward discontinuity in the development of business procedures. Thus their widening application to problems of this kind places a very large and hitherto unprecedented responsibility upon the manufacturer and purveyor of the equipment as well as upon its ultimate user.

Equipment maintenance

As a result of the uniqueness of the digital computer—in terms of both its engineering and its application—from the development of the very first such machine continuously and increasingly to the present time, the maintenance of the equipment has come to be the almost exclusive responsibility of its manufacturer. Such a responsibility does not of course go uncompensated; hence the (usually high) estimated cost of equipment maintenance has become a regular part of its rental cost and in most cases long-term maintenance contracts are a standard adjunct to the outright purchase agreements between user and computer manufacturer.

Most manufacturers are surprisingly conscientious about this very significant responsibility. They have to be. Their future sales depend on it. Some manufacturers of computers have successfully sold their product not on its technological merits but on the reputation of the product and the manufacturer for high reliability and effective maintenance practices.

Although inadequate maintenance practices by the manufacturer are not entirely unknown under contracts where the equipment is rented or leased by the user from the manufacturer, the threat of almost immediate cancellation of this contract is a strong deterrent to the continuation of such practices. The situation is quite similar in those cases where the equipment has been purchased by the user and is maintained by the manufacturer under a contract specifically for this purpose.

The financial advantage to the user of equipment maintenance is not always in favor of the manufacturer doing it. Whereas the maintenance costs cannot be explicitly and positively identified in those cases where the equipment is rented, they are automatically so identified where a special maintenance contract exists. In some cases they have been found to be excessively high. In a few such cases, it has proved advantageous to the user to develop his own maintenance capability, either by hiring competent engineers and training them appropriately or actually by "pirating" engineers from the manufacturer when the time is ripe by offering very large salaries and other inducements. Even though this may involve substantial dollar costs to the user, savings as high as 50 per cent over the maintenance contract offered by the manufacturer have been reported. But this is the exception rather than the rule.

The importance of maintenance is ever-increasing. At today's rates of up to $1 for a single minute of operation, and at tomorrow's rates of $100 or more a minute, it is sometimes necessary to resort to rather extreme measures to prevent extended periods of machine breakdown. The resultant trend has been to introduce engineering refinements into the computer design specifically for the purpose of increasing its ability to operate without malfunction or automatically to detect such malfunctions when they occur. This policy has resulted in the production of some computers which are among the most highly reliable complex devices ever built. Its almost certain continuance is likely to result in essentially "fail-safe" equipment of the highest order.

On the whole, therefore, it seems that the computer manufacturer has accepted his responsibility for equipment maintenance well. He has increasingly included reliability considerations in his designs, and he has provided on-the-job maintenance service of the utmost skill and availability as a routine contractual matter. As this problem increases with the growing complexity of computing equipment, it will be his role to improve his ability to maintain the equipment at a pace adequate to meet the challenge. On the basis of past experience, he can with some confidence be expected to do this.

CHAPTER 8

Problems of Transition

As AN INDIVIDUAL increases his experience and competence in the solution of business data processing problems, an important shift occurs in the kind of problems he attacks. This individual progresses, ideally, from performing routine operations according to fairly well specified rules to the far more complex job of organizing his data and rules and deciding upon a suitable course of action according to the dictates of this information supplemented by his judgment and experience. Thus the individual progresses toward the use of increasingly complex criteria to solve his problems.

Increasing experience with the application of data processing equipment to business-type problems suggests that a similar transition must take place in the use of this equipment. The manipulation of data according to increasingly complex criteria seems certainly to be the destiny of the computer. Although we must avoid *creating* complex criteria *because* we have computers available, their application in those situations where complex criteria are *essential* to success is likely to become widespread.

Unfortunately, not all the problems associated with this

transition are logical; some are organizational, some sociological, some economic, some philosophical, and some
psychological. All these problems are created by the transition from a data processing system which solves only the
routine repetitive jobs at hand to one which deals effectively
with all the relevant data and complex business criteria.
Some of them are discussed on the following pages.

The digital computer, as we have indicated, is capable of
executing very complex operations; in most cases, it is most
efficiently utilized when it is so employed. Likewise, the data
processing effort which must occur in support of a business
operation is not only complex in many respects but is often
defined only subtly or not explicitly defined at all, even as
it is carried out. Our problem then may be stated as that of
dealing with the barrier between the operating management
of a business organization and the designers and operators
of the computer system which supports it.

To date this barrier has been difficult to bridge. As a
consequence there may result in the extreme, when a computer is installed, a transfer of the operating control of an
organization from the management charged with the responsibility for such control to the computer organization
which was never intended to exercise it. At the other extreme, management can retain nominal control over the
data processing operation centered at the computer by
allowing the inertia of that operation to incorporate many
of the ill-defined aspects of the antiquated operating system into the newly designed system of the computer, thus
perpetuating the need for human intervention in the operating system.

The transitional problems thus created are in part those of communication between management on the one hand and the computer (and its agents) on the other. Again it is a problem of people. The people trained in the understanding of computers are (usually) untrained in the operations of the business; the people experienced in the day-to-day operating problems of the business are (more usually) inexperienced in the techniques involved in planning and operating a computer system in a business environment. For this reason, people with a large fund of knowledge concerning the business functions are unable to inject this knowledge into the computer-system development, and people with valuable experience in computer operations cannot make the corresponding contribution for which their background qualifies them.

Throughout this book, we have discussed the use of the digital computer in what we have called the business data processing environment. As the operations of the digital computer in this environment become increasingly complex, the scope of the relationship of the computer to its environment increases correspondingly. Conversely, each of the complex computer operations tends to extend over the domain of several organizations within the firm, thereby broadening the sphere of influence of each.

As long as the data processing operations remain segmented into logically simple, functionally separate jobs, the environment with which each deals remains correspondingly simple. With the introduction of the computer, integrated data processing operations, each dealing with several areas of business, become not only feasible but often desirable. Thus in each of its many functional activities, the digital computer is properly the servant of many masters. Its products are specified, often in conflicting fashion, by the controller and the sales manager alike; and its schedules are competed for by the personnel manager and the inventory manager. As the tool of integration, the computer system faces the problem of defining the inconsistencies among essentially autonomous elements of business management. To the extent that we utilize its capability to integrate the operations of a business organization into a meaningful whole, a digital computer system creates an environment totally new to the business world.

The revisions associated with the introduction of such a digital computer system are often quite substantial, in terms of organization, responsibility, and attitudes. That the benefit of all may mean the detriment of some becomes self-evident as integration occurs. But in the final analysis, it is the loss of prestige and apparent authority that is probably the major cause of management difficulties in the transition to the computer system of a modern business environment.

The computer antagonizes existing procedures

In most of the examples representing experience to date, the decision to install a digital computer system is made in the presence of existing procedures. Some day it is possible that techniques of scientific management may have advanced to such an extent that the operation of a profitable business without the assistance of a computer system from the outset will be a practical impossibility. But for the present, existing systems seem likely to remain a major stumbling block. The problem of transition to a digital computer system is therefore characterized by the need to break away from existing mores rather than to establish entirely new ones in the absence of any existing business culture.

But can it be said, once for all, what is the *really* best decision-making plan with which to replace the old and to which to apply the newly introduced digital computer system? We think not. Any decision-making plan—even a bad one—involves the identification of the points in the organization at which decisions are made, along with the specification of the information necessary at each point to make them. Such a plan has proved to be not a single plan but a highly dynamic sequence of plans. While it is the purpose of the data processing system to provide the right information at the right place at the right time, the dynamic aspects of what is truly right are such as to dictate an ever-changing data processing system.

When, then, can we stop to introduce the computer as a tool? It seems clear that, if we wait for the "best" decision-making plan to be determined, our opportunity will never arrive. Whatever our plan for decision making at a particular time, it is not the best. Therefore, as a practical matter, we must utilize our newly devised computer system to implement a decision-making plan which we know to be imperfect. At this time, to be sure, we can and should introduce whatever improvements in the decision-making plan we have been able to develop. Such a procedure, coming as it does at a discontinuous point in the execution of decisions

of the organization, provides the opportunity to avoid the
perpetuation of those aspects of the plan which have proved
to be undesirable and to introduce those changes in that
plan which are believed to be advantageous.

It is clear, in a complex business data processing system,
that while changes made at this opportunity may be very
large, subsequent changes of equal size and importance are
likely to be required. Therefore it is most important that the
newly introduced data processing system be oriented to
ever-changing conditions to the maximum extent possible.
Only by this means can we chart a course which is at least
directed toward the continued improvement in the efficiency
of complex business data processing operations.

Psychological Barriers to Automatic Decision Making.
Psychologists tell us that, according to the theory of work
group leaders, a requirement that a group function effectively as a group is that the group be provided with a leader
capable of organizing the activities of the group toward a
common end. To a certain extent, the computer has assumed
the role of the leader, and to this extent, it is substantially
incapable of fulfilling its psychological role.

Whereas the various logical operations necessary to establish the decisions reached have in the past always been
readily traceable by members of the group, the use of a
large-scale digital computer as a tool of the system has
made this no longer possible. For this reason, the human
members of the group tend to suspect those operations and
decisions, however explicitly prespecified, which they do
not understand (or at least cannot readily trace). The
psychological barrier created is in many ways more real and

important than the technological one of utilizing entirely new equipment in the business data processing field.

An interesting example of this phenomenon is given by a recent experience in the insurance field. It is the position of some of our insurance agents that it is they to whom their particular segment of the business ultimately belongs and that it should therefore be they who manage every aspect of the conduct of that particular business. Insurance agents often feel, further, that there is a great deal of judgment and experience involved in the sale and maintenance of an individual account, and that this judgment and experience cannot be prespecified to the extent that it can be programmed for a computer. We have no reason to quarrel with these points of view.

This example, however, characterizes this precomputer problem very well indeed. We find that this problem is characterized by a very significant state of confusion between the management *control* over a data processing task and the *execution* of that task. Stemming from the period during which the execution of data processing tasks was accomplished by essentially manual procedural systems, this position, which was certainly applicable then, is not necessarily applicable in the environment of today and even less so in the expected environment of the future. As pride in one's job rears its ugly (from an efficient data processing point of view) head, further confusion exists as to whether certain data processing tasks of each agent are sufficiently "simple" (i.e., definable, well specified, and determinable with the data at hand) to be carried out by automatic equipment, or whether the judgment and experience of the agent are an indispensable aspect of every data processing operation of the system.

Thus failing to distinguish sharply between the *efficient accomplishment* of a data processing job and the *responsibility* for the accomplishment of that job may lead to a situation in which everyone is reluctant to adapt the digital computer to his daily operations, even though his problems are eminently well suited to such treatment. Similarly, the insistence on the existence of broad areas of "class knowledge," dependent upon subtleties learned of experience and not easily definable in logical terms tends to subdue efforts to introduce logical definitions into areas where its need is vital.

Great Expectations. Modern large-scale computer operations in business today are almost invariably characterized by great expectations on the part of management at the time the plan to initiate them becomes a fact. The point on which we must be clear is that the nature of these great expectations remains fuzzy and unclear in many cases. Is the gain expected to be in terms of savings in operating costs and, if so, what kind? Is the gain related to "better management" and, if so, in what way is it expected to be better?

There are unfortunately a great many situations in which a computer system is introduced into the data processing operations of a firm because of a general attitude on the part of its management that the effectiveness of the data processing job is far less than it should be, and a vague feeling that new electronic data processing devices are superior to the older manual or electromechanical means. When this happens, the management responsible for the introduction of the machine is almost sure to be disappointed in the results.

But we have also found that expectations are sometimes underdone. In the recent history of digital computer applications there now can be found many instances in which the installation of a digital computer system has proved to be far more effective than was ever anticipated—even by the computer manufacturer at whose insistence the computer was installed.

These applications have achieved such success in ways that could not be (or at least were not) expected. One company was able to eliminate the odd change from its regular payroll disbursements and, by reducing its payroll force accordingly, was able to save a full month's rental of the computer each year. Another organization was able to gain control of the appropriations for its various departments and thus eliminate departmental competition and excessive financial commitments and in general enforce the financial program intended by the original budget. A third firm was able to process transactions for its clearinghouse so much more rapidly than by its previous methods that the interest saved was enough to offset the rental costs of half of the entire computer installation. Still another organization was able to meet a requirement to double the size of its inventory in a single year, to increase the number of retail outlets, and to handle as many as four times the normal number of transactions against that inventory without falling behind in its operations, incurring overtime costs, or taxing its data processing capabilities in any way.

Even today, the list of savings in unexpected ways due to digital computers is almost endless. Then too, as our experience in the application of digital computers to business problems continues to grow at an ever-increasing rate, the instance in which very great expectations of computer operation are realized is becoming commonplace. This happy state of affairs is due both to growing capabilities and numbers of computer specialists and to the growing understanding and confidence of business management. Dictating as it does an increasing confidence in business data processing, this development is one of the most favorable which can be detected in the field.

Today one can be almost certain that the degree of success of one's computer installation will not be what one expects; it will be either substantially better or significantly poorer. In a decade or two (or three or four), a digital computer installation will represent a business tool whose place in the operations has become as certain as that of the time clock, the printing press, or the milling machine.

Effects of transition on the individual

Labor, Management, and Computers. Revealing itself increasingly as a potential deterrent to the onset of the widespread automatic processing of data in business organizations is another problem which is not technological but sociological in nature. This is the management problem of identifying and coping with the true impact of automatic data processing devices on that portion of the labor force currently employed in carrying out these operations. Although a great many aspects of this problem are beyond the scope of this book (and the knowledge of the writer), let us discuss some of the more important aspects which have come to our attention.

For the most part, the people who are likely to be affected directly by the introduction of data processing equipment in business operations are not well informed in the field of data processing. Thus these people, dealing with a field in which they are actually laymen, are at once fascinated with and apprehensive of the oncoming data processing technology.

It is the usual attitude of people to exalt technological change. It seems fundamentally desirable to seek such change since it is an important aspect of continuing progress on the American scene. While in the past the impact on society of almost every such change seemed relatively insignificant when the change was first introduced, the potential impact on society of the introduction of automatic data processing equipment seems even now to be incomprehensibly large. Thus the expected magnitude of the sociological impact creates the attitudes of both awe and trepidation with which the coming data processing technology is held.

There are basically two ways in which this apprehension manifests itself in the minds and attitudes of the present data processing labor force. The first is a fear of job displacement, loss of job security, or of intellectual inadequacy to operate in this unfamiliar environment. The second is the fear that some measure of operating control will be lost by assigning tasks to an automatic device for execution and hence that these devices will somehow be unable to consider the effects on the working individual of the tasks they accomplish and the decisions they make.

An important corollary of this great concern on the part of labor at the advance of an automatic data processing technology is that it occurs at a time when labor is very well organized and consequently at a time when the views of labor are likely to have a substantial impact on the course of events. Such was not the case, for example, when the automobile was first introduced into our society or the sewing machine or the cotton gin or any other technological advances representative of the so-called "industrial revolution."

Although automatic data processing is certainly the least reprehensible example of automation possible from a labor point of view, it is nevertheless subject to the attitudes on automation which prevail in organized labor. The union movement in America today is on record in favor of the eventual introduction of automation into business activities. It is clear that increased automation can lead (and already has lead) to shorter working hours, increased leisure time, and a substantial increase in consumer purchasing power. But it is clear that it is the objective of automation to eliminate people from jobs and replace them with machines. While it can be argued over the long run that the net effect will be to create higher-skill higher-paying jobs in the automated industries, and simultaneously to create a large class of totally new jobs in the new industry of automation, this circumstance cannot compensate for the immediate unfavorable impact on the individuals in the existing labor force. Even the promised long-range improvement in the nation's over-all economy cannot correct earlier hardships which automation might induce.

It is not surprising then that the very labor organizations which are on record in favor of the introduction of automation into business in the future are substantially opposed to its widespread introduction now. This resistance to change is based on the obvious potential hardships to people whose present occupations will be replaced or substantially altered by automatic processing. Unanswered questions include: whether the firm or the individual should bear the expense of retraining these people, whether the salary rate of an individual should be permitted to decrease when job positions have been changed from responsible ones to junior ones by the new technology, and whether general salary rates should be increased so as to compensate for reductions in workdays made possible by automatic devices.

Pertaining largely to operations like production lines in factories rather than to the operations of processing data, the economic arguments on the general question of automation, advanced by both management and labor, are legion. Labor's view that overproductivity must be reduced by decreasing the number of working hours without decreasing the purchasing power, and hence the corresponding wages, is contrasted with management's view that apparent overproductivity will result in greater demand as well as in lower prices, and hence in a healthier economy. Here again we wish merely to suggest that the answers to these questions are not intuitively obvious and that the answers in the data processing field must await the accumulation of a considerable fund of experience.

Concurrently with the consideration of management responsibility to the individuals in its labor force when that force is disrupted, we must similarly scrutinize the activities of organized labor in this regard. The responsibility for the welfare of individuals during and after a period of technological advance must certainly be shared by labor with management.

Labor unions today have taken it upon themselves to maintain a great knowledge of the problems and promise of the particular industry with which each deals so that they may better understand and cope with the problems that arise. By the same criteria, it seems clear that these unions should undertake to study in detail the potential impact of automatic data processing on their organization and its members and further to carry out such a study on a continuing basis utilizing persons familiar with the problems of data processing and who have the special skills involved therein. Only by such an approach can the unions develop and maintain a knowledgeable attitude on the automation of data processing in business firms.

There is also the matter of narrowness of scope. While it may prove to be a demonstrable fact that the widespread introduction of automatic data processing equipment in a certain industry will reduce the number of data processing jobs available in that industry, it may also be true that such a move will so increase the number of jobs available outside this industry—and consequently outside the immediate interests of the union—that the net effect will represent an improvement rather than a degradation of the labor situation.

And finally, of course, labor, like management, is apprehensive of the oncoming era of automatic data processing because the technology and techniques involved are not fully understood in either camp. It seems therefore the direct responsibility of labor, just as it is of management, to act so as to inform itself adequately of the true facts of the case. That an arbitrary, totalitarian, impersonal management will develop as a result of employing computers as a management tool is probably no more likely than that computers will cause management to become increasingly logical, democratic, and sensitive to individual problems.

The matter of potential job displacement by automatic data processing techniques has still another aspect. It is probably true that the rapidity with which automation seems to come, even in a particular case, is more apparent than real. Contrary to what most management people think (perhaps because they would like to think so), programs to introduce automatic data processing techniques and equipment are not characterized by overnight improvements when the program is implemented. For this reason, the problem of job displacement is far less than it may seem to be at first glance. It has been demonstrated that normal attrition of a clerical staff can often be described by a figure of 30 to 40 per cent of that staff on an annual basis. Such staffs, containing as they do a very large percentage of female employees, are usually maintained in such a way that normal attrition is more than adequate to deal with any reduction or reassignment of personnel which may result.[1]

---

[1] It should further be noted in passing that instances wherein the total labor force (connected with the data processing activity before the

There are a great many interesting examples of the impact of digital computers on labor-management relationships to be found in the literature. A most interesting activity of this kind, which the author has not seen related previously, deals with an operation which is operationally small but extremely critical in nature: the calculation of the odds at a racetrack following each racing event of the day.

The payments for win, place, and show—the odds, in other words—corresponding to the result of each race run are computed by highly skilled professional people employed by the racetrack and known as "calculators." These computations must occur very soon after the completion of the race, usually before the results have been declared "official," to permit the odds to be posted as soon as possible so that the winning public can be paid and the losing public can commiserate with itself. It is obvious that any delay in the normal procedures would meet with the unanimous disfavor of the public and management alike and therefore cannot be tolerated.

Consider then the insertion of a digital computer into this environment. While such a device is likely to be more rapid and accurate than its human counterparts when it is operating properly, it is a *device* and is therefore apparently subject to periods of malfunction. Whereas for an eight-race daily program the machine is required for a total time of

---

computer system was installed) has been significantly reduced in number (after that installation) are very few indeed. What is often found in these cases is that the data processing organization is now able to accomplish so much more analysis to assist management in planning that a force consisting of both the people employed in the precomputer system and the people added to man the computer activity is required.

only about 15 minutes, this machine time must be accumulated during the period immediately following each race. It is possible that at some time during these particular 15 minutes a malfunction would occur.

A decision must therefore be made as to whether a computer and an appropriate set of procedures for pretesting the device and postchecking the results will be utilized or whether the human "calculators" with error rates perhaps 100 or 1,000 times as great but with long-established (but nonetheless not infallible) procedures for checking results will be retained for the job.

With the promise of entirely automatic, completely checked operation, the computer seems to management to be the more desirable path to take. The labor organization representing the "calculators" takes a very strong stand in favor of the retention of these people on the basis of their vast experience (beginning only about two decades ago) in the job. Such an impasse, resulting as it does in the inability to utilize the special skills of the "calculators" in the development of the computer operations, seems unreasonably to delay the close of the transitional period from manual to automatic operation.

Individuals, Organization, and Computers. It has been observed that the psychological advancement of man continues over the months, over the years, and over the centuries at a much slower pace than does the technological advancement which surrounds him. The introduction of a digital computer system into a business environment is certainly more of a psychological problem than are the design and construction of the devices used in the system. Let us consider then a few of the kinds of psychological problems which these computers create.

The problem of the definition of goals—or at least agreement as to which goals represent the basic purpose of any business firm—is surely fundamental. We have suggested this earlier in this volume. We suggested further [2] that it might in fact be truly impossible clearly and unambiguously to define a set of goals for a business organization which are acceptable to all concerned.

This dilemma may provide a reason why the technology of digital computers has thus far been able to outstrip the art and science of their application; i.e., the relative difficulty of defining goals is far greater in the area of computer applications to business problems than it is in the area of designing and building the devices themselves. Furthermore, while people have often been able to choose, intuitively or logically, the better of two goals offered to them, it has not always been possible to specify how precisely to achieve the preferred goal by applying data processing techniques to the problem. The dual difficulty—increased over that associated with the engineering technology involved—of identifying the most desirable goals and achieving them once they have been identified is probably the main aspect of business data processing which distinguishes it from other problems encountered in the commercial world.

To see one's way through this maze of difficulties is indeed a difficult task. The system designer must not only be familiar with and sympathetic toward the many varied skills (of both a business and a computing nature) involved in

[2] Chapter 3.

the application of data processing techniques to business problems, but it is also necessary for him to be equipped to resolve rationally rather than emotionally the controversies which are inevitable in the design of these applications.

The skills which must be those of a successful system *designer* are not necessarily the same as those of an expert in *managing* a data processing system, a system of production, or a system of budgeting, once such a system has been designed and is in operation. The "toughness" vital to the operating function can be largely misplaced in the developmental one. Dedication to an announced purpose is fundamental to managing an organization but dangerous when carried to an extreme in designing a data processing system.

As system design is completed, some of the special skills associated with the development of a data processing system of new design must be replaced by certain other important special skills required to operate the new systems. These skills of operation are special because of the key role which must be played by *people* in a system in which most of the operations are performed automatically, as is the case in a system involving a large-scale digital computer system. To the extent that the errors committed by people in a highly automated system cannot be both detected and corrected automatically, the efficiency of that automatic system is reduced to the level of efficiency of the manual intervention required to accomplish this error detection and correction.

Thus every effort must be bent toward minimizing the errors allowed to enter the system. Under error-free circumstances, for example, the calculation of gross to net pay for an entire payroll might require only 2 or 3 minutes of computer time. But, if as few as ten errors of the type described above are allowed to enter the system, this same calculation might consume a full hour.

These considerations emphasize the importance of people in a highly mechanized data processing system. Their role is a vital one in operation as well as in design. For this reason, it seems clear that the training, adaptability, and attitudes required of data processing personnel in a computer-oriented system must be quite different, and usually quite superior, to those now considered necessary in the noncomputer field of data processing.

The transition of our business society

It is characteristic of society in general and of the business community in particular to be unable to comprehend at any given time the magnitude of increased capability gained over a long-range passage of time. The very rapid advance of the data processing field within the past decade has served to magnify this problem manyfold.

Likewise it is true that, while individuals tend to exhibit a well-known reluctance to change their concepts and procedures, business organizations and other groups display an even greater inertia in this regard.

The newness, the high promise, and the demonstrated value of the digital computer in a business environment have all been important factors in the rapid expansion of its use. It is perhaps unfortunate that the introduction of this new tool into this vast field has not dictated a corresponding change in ideas about concepts and procedures.

This difficulty is not peculiar to the computer field. It

might also be characterized as a continuing conflict between historical or traditional motives on the one hand and logical or scientific motives on the other. Thus described, it is easy to see that we have had the problem as long as we have been dealing with planned procedures. No operations based on planned procedures can be introduced into a social vacuum and hence it is necessary that their design consider the existing environment and the nontechnical problems attendant thereto.

Observe, moreover, that the reverse problem is also at hand. Over the long run, a high degree of automation can introduce into day-to-day activities what we now would consider an undesirably high degree of *conformity*. Thus our banking activities may become highly regimented, our tax-paying procedures fixed, our transportation efforts tightly scheduled, and our economic attitudes stereotyped. This conformity effect is amplified by the fact that man tends first to automate those procedures which formerly were highly manual, i.e., procedural systems which were densely populated by people and therefore highly subjective, individualistic, and correspondingly nonconformist. Attacking these areas first—while desirable from several points of view—tends to create a transitional upheaval far greater than would the choice of areas of machine application amenable to relatively objective analysis, relatively new to the data processing field, and of more direct benefit to management than to daily operations.

In the half dozen years during which the application of digital computer systems to business has been introduced and become known, only about one of twenty firms whose size and complexity is such as to warrant the use of computers has actually seen fit to use them. More startling, perhaps, is the fact that only about 10 per cent of the firms which used some lesser form of nonmanual data processing —on punched cards, for example—have undergone the conversion of their semimanual systems to systems involving large computer facilities.

One of the main hurdles to be overcome in this regard is that of informing both workers and management of the *facts* about automatic data processing equipment and techniques. Poorly informed people tend to "supplement" their information by their own experience or by logical deduction if they possibly can do so. Often they make money doing it. The resultant bad counseling is likely to produce an erroneous management picture of the computer field, since the popular experiences in and deductions about this field are often inaccurate to a most unusual extent.

Newspapers and books have been largely responsible for this situation, although the equipment manufacturers are not without blame. Cartoons depict computers as the intellectual superiors of men, science fiction expounds on the vast capabilities of computers, and advertisements relate the ease with which computers can assume the clerical duties involved in extensive business operations. Experience in the field provides one with some basis on which to interpret this humor, fiction, or cajolery, but the layman without the benefit of such experience is likely to be influenced erroneously.

Indeed, some of the people who engage in the deception are themselves laymen, have so been deceived, and are merely passing on unwittingly their honest but erroneous impressions of computerdom. Other instances of the deception are not quite so coincidental. The literature of the workingman is sprinkled with articles "warning" him of the onset of automation. While these articles often include a report of some advantages of automation to workers in the long run, more often these workers are led to believe that they must sacrifice themselves to automation to gain these advantages for future generations.

Probably the main comment which may be made about all this is that, while the potential advantages of automatic data processing are rarely overstated, in fact or in jest, the *ease* with which these advantages may be achieved *almost always is*. In the future, and probably within our lifetime, computers will store prodigious files of information with instant access, carry out computations of almost any complexity with lightning speed, and carry out the logical procedures necessary to operate large complex business organizations. But to achieve all this, *people* must construct and maintain the equipment to carry it out, they must identify and procure the information to be stored in the files, they must specify in every detail the computations required, and they must determine or agree upon logical procedures which will govern the operations of these firms. The jobs of engineering, identifying, procuring, specifying, and determining these things require a vast force of manpower on an ever-increasing basis.

Even as the advance of computers into our society faces as its greatest difficulty the widespread misinformation concerning it, so does this same advance offer as its greatest potential advantage the enlightenment of man. In the short space of time during which computers have been available for man's use, he has begun to contemplate and even achieve intellectual adventures inconceivable to his predecessors. Giant technological strides are now possible on theoretical grounds which could not have been established a decade ago without the computer as a logical and mathematical tool. Modern atomic power, jet aircraft, and space travel suggest only some of the present and future advances achieved in this manner. The extension of the fields of social science into mathematics and logic has already had a major impact on our environment.

In the final chapter of this book, we have attempted to report some of the activities of this nature which have already been accomplished, as well as others which are currently in the development stages. It is obvious that many of both kinds have been omitted from this report and that others with perhaps far greater impacts on society are totally unknown today. This report indicates, nevertheless, some of the nature and scope of today's effort in this vital matter.

CHAPTER 9

The Present Bespeaks the Future

BECAUSE THE DIGITAL computer has developed so rapidly, the opportunity to develop a sound fund of knowledge which would adequately describe it to the general public has been reduced substantially. Thus *existing* computer applications are reported as though they were entirely foreign to our normal form of operation, and the reported scope of *planned* computer applications is often amplified out of all relation to the facts.

In the recent past it has been observed that the technological aspects of these machines do not represent the primary basis for this barrier to understanding them but rather that it is a certain flair for the bizarre on the part of those who represent them to the public which has resulted in the exaggerations which abound. That computers have failed to live up to their advertising in some cases may be the fault of the advertising rather than the computers. The reasons for this are many and varied: Manufacturers wish their product to be as awe-inspiring as possible; users wish their management and their public to regard highly their efforts at modernization; and reporters of events involving digital computers, understanding neither the details of the events involved nor the role of the computer in them, tend to overstate both.

A current development in the field has been the growing desire to introduce into business data processing the theories and techniques of scientific management and operations research now being developed in laboratories across the nation. Integration of sales with sales commissions, accounts receivable, customer billing, credit, production control, and finished-parts inventories, has become an important goal of business management. These promising theories, mostly unproved in actual practice, tend to extend the scope of the resultant automatic data processing into functional integration and management decision making far beyond the present understanding of the lay public. Employed merely as tools which enable the contemplation and implementation of these concepts, computers and their prowess have become hopelessly confused with the *theories* of advanced management whose implementation the machines make possible.

The future cannot be predicted accurately, for its true nature is obscured even from those whose purposes it is to establish it. We can, however—and indeed, we must—endeavor to determine the trends which seem to be under way. Only by doing so can we hope to develop a reasonable set of goals toward which to work and by which to measure our subsequent progress.

Let us discuss some developments in the field of data processing as they apply to computers and related hardware. In this discussion we shall attempt to clarify the distinction between data processing itself and the new management concepts it makes possible. Some of these developments, existing as they do in today's environment, portend an impact far greater than their present one on future environments. Other developments, in process or planned for future implementation, may produce an impact on our business society in excess of any we can presently contemplate.

The climate for growth

Notwithstanding a recent economic recession and considerable talk about a lengthy leveling-off period, it seems clear that the economy of the United States is growing in size and complexity at the present time and will continue to do so for the foreseeable future. As a direct result of such growth characteristics as a population increase, a general shift to an industrial-type economy, and a very significant trend toward increasingly complex government regulations, the work load in data processing seems continually on the increase. Contributory factors of Federal origin include social security, unemployment insurance, wage and hour requirements, interstate commerce regulations, Federal Reserve rules, Security and Exchange Commission controls, Treasury Department regulations, etc.

Along with this continued growth in our national economy we have experienced a steady increase in the total number of clerical workers, an increase in the percentage of the total working force they represent, and an increase in their salary in real dollars. Providing ever-increasing material abundance as well as increased leisure for individual creative and recreational pursuits, our economy has developed a climate which only continued improvement can sustain. For the clerical problem—and for clerical workers and management alike—the development of digital computer hardware and techniques seems the only way to achieve this.

To most large companies, potential benefits from the implementation of new or vastly better management techniques for accomplishing company objectives has begun to dominate any dollar savings in clerical areas made possible by modern data processing equipment. Increasing efficiency of American firms and stepped-up competition from foreign sources (due to transportation and communication improvements as well as the general advance of those economies) is beginning to create a situation in which only the most efficient operations and only the most advanced techniques of management can survive.

But in this rush toward automation that we have suggested, it is clear that not every company is large and complex enough to automate its clerical operations. Numerous firms are small enough that they can maintain a high rate of efficiency and even introduce those newly developed techniques of scientific management which would benefit them without the aid of any digital computer (although *some* automatic data processing equipment might be useful). Thus theirs is a convenient solution to the data processing problem.

There are, finally, those companies of what we might call the "awkward" size. Not large enough to support a full-time digital computer system, they are too large to overlook the advantages which might be gleaned from the utilization of modern data processing techniques in their operations.

These firms too are provided with a rather convenient class of solutions to this apparent dilemma: the part-time use of a computer leased or owned by another company, the employment of the facilities of a computer service center on an "as-needed" basis, or participation in a cooperative group established for the purpose of making computing facilities available to its members.

Thus the climate for the growth of digital computer systems in our total economy as well as in many individual firms is highly favorable. The growing number of successful applications is an important further stimulus in this direction. If a representative can be found at today's meetings of bankers or merchants or manufacturers who does not now already operate or plan to utilize a digital computer system, that representative is almost certain to hold the view that his firm will be moving toward the advantageous utilization of a digital computer some time in the future.

Experts have predicted that the total United States capacity to process data will increase to twenty or thirty times the present value by 1965 and to more than 100 times the present value by 1970. The combination of increasingly capable computers in increasing numbers and most of all of improved techniques for their utilization makes even this estimate sound conservative to some.

This increase in equipment capability in the data processing field can be described in terms of four major areas: increased automation of data preparation and communication, vastly increased capacity to store information in readily accessible form, major increases in the speed of data manipulation within the computer, and improved output devices capable of reflecting processed results in an increasingly useful and timely form. Continued improvement in these four areas, in part a result of experience gained in the field, is truly basic to continued improvement in business data processing.

The application of digital computers to current problems

Perhaps the best way to illustrate the impact of the digital computer on our way of life is to describe in terms of that way of life some applications in which these devices have been or are planned to be utilized. These applications, impinging as they do on our everyday activities, will illustrate the very significant way in which the digital computer is affecting and will affect our business society. Some idea of the scope of this impact in our daily activities can also be gained from these examples.

Individual Tax Returns. Several applications exist today in which a digital computer is utilized to recompute on behalf of the official agency involved the tax computation previously carried out by the taxpayer. This recomputation involves the income figures reported by the taxpayer. Its purpose is to check in a completely impartial fashion the computations carried out by the taxpayer. By making possible the very rapid and accurate checking of these returns (prepared by you and me), the machine enables the diversion of experienced personnel from routine work which formerly occupied a substantial portion of their time to other work which cannot be automated.

Sales Recording and Analysis in the Retail Store. A recent development in the operational use of digital computer systems has been a device which automatically reads and records (in a form suitable for automatic data processing) the information represented by a ticket attached to a piece of merchandise in a retail store. This development represents an impact on the entire consumer population. It enables the store to accumulate data regarding the merchandise sold (size, price, color, lot, etc.), and thereby to study the sales trends exhibited, the budget commitments made or required, and the stock replenishment actions indicated by the sales made. As a result of this ability, the store is in a position to give better service to the customer and hence to maximize its profits as compared with the competition in the long run.

The merchandise ticket involved in this particular example has been a small piece of cardboard punched with pinlike holes which reflect in coded form the required information. In the future it will be possible to print this information directly on the tag and to read it directly by magnetic or photoelectric means. At the time when it is read, this information can be recorded in a medium which allows it to be entered into a digital computer. The computer then carries out the indicated analysis according to its programmed instructions.

The obvious advantages of these techniques are in some measure offset by several factors. Probably the largest single such factor is that, in most large retail organizations operating today, a great amount of capital has already been invested in the equipment presently used to record the transactions which take place, e.g., cash registers. As a result of this, a strong reluctance on the part of store operators to install new equipment, and thus make the old obsolete, is encountered. Limitations of this and many other kinds, imposed by the existing environment into which the new system must be thrust, are common today wherever new systems are to be installed.

The Credit Card. Substantially limited to oil companies and a few hotels and restaurants during the period preceding World War II, the credit card business is now emerging in its own right as an important United States industry. Employed as expense account records, user activity monitors, and records for explaining business expenses on income tax returns, the billings resulting from the use of these cards portend a major new area for the application of modern data processing equipment and techniques.

Until recently, most of the credit card billing activity was carried out without the benefit of modern digital computers. But the broadening of the scope of business to which credit card techniques have been extended, and the burgeoning rosters of members of credit organizations have caused the credit activity and hence the credit problem to increase tenfold in the past decade.

The problem is a straightforward one of collecting the data from the member firms, handling and organizing the data at hand, and periodically billing the customers and paying the business organizations with which the credit card firm deals on the basis of these data. The information reflecting the relevant events which have taken place must be entered by the member firm's regular clerk at the time the purchase is made. Since these persons are not trained and experienced in special recording techniques, the recording of the data must be simplified to the greatest extent possible. The objective in this key input area must be to maximize the extent to which these data, which are the basis of the entire system, are accurate and complete.

Much of the information describing the transaction which has taken place can be recorded automatically. Metal name plates and plastic cards with raised letters indicating the name of the customer have already been widely used, and devices are now being developed and tested which will permit the information so recorded to be read automatically, again by magnetic or photoelectric means. The use of such techniques, together with those for entering information about the item purchased, will mean that only the dollar amount of the transaction need be entered manually by the clerk representing the member firm. Further steps, introduced to automate most of even this operation, will ensure the competitive position of the credit firm utilizing them.

Pay Television. Not yet operational on any wide scale in our present society, the imminent onset of pay TV presents a data processing problem of the first magnitude. This problem is not entirely dissimilar to the one described above, except perhaps that it may be larger in volume. It is not unlikely, for example, that a single city of moderate size will represent several hundred thousand subscribers to a pay TV service. An extension of these figures reveals that a weekly billing of perhaps 10 million events for a single pay TV firm is not at all out of the question. In New York City alone, the number of daily transactions may approach that amount.

In an application of this sheer magnitude, it seems that

some advanced form of data processing is an absolute requirement to the efficient accomplishment of the customer
billing. From this very real standpoint, the implementation
of pay TV in the private homes of individuals is seen to be
a technological problem not of the television equipment but
of the data processing techniques involved.

"Customer Favor" Applications. Emerging from the lab-
yrinth of data processing applications is a rather large
class of applications whose *primary* purpose has been to
gain or renew "customer favor" in the business firm employing them. These customer-oriented applications are usually
concerned with providing faster, less expensive, or more
accurate service to the customer wherever he requires it.

Large warehouses stocking items which may be needed
on very short notice have applied modern techniques of
data processing—especially that of random access to large
files of information stored electronically—to considerable
advantage to their customer. Examples can be found where
the "customer" is represented by a private individual, another firm, or even another division of the firm maintaining
the warehouse. Mail-order houses, grocery-store chains, and
spare-parts warehouses for household items are very likely
the most common examples of this application.

The impact of applications of this type can be observed
in many different ways. In many cases, a reduction in the
total inventories required to support the warehousing activity has been reported. In other cases, the major advantage
has been to improve the competitive position of the warehouse user by making the contents of the warehouse avail-

able to him far more rapidly than those of competing warehouses.

In the vast majority of cases of this type, important advantages have accrued to both the customer and the warehouser. These advantages have been in terms of improved service to the customer and a corresponding increase in the effectiveness of the warehousing endeavors. Illustrative of these gains are the reduction of sales losses to competitors due to an out-of-stock condition, order refilling measured in terms of hours rather than days (when an out-of-stock condition does occur), and the resultant ability of the customer to maintain relatively low inventory levels and thereby to minimize the risk of inventory obsolescence so often dominant in fast-changing product lines.

Increased Utilization of Business Capital. Many examples today reflect the increased recognition of the value to a business organization of a rapid turnover of capital or stock. Because the digital computer makes possible the analysis of a financial or an inventory position at very short time intervals—daily, for example—it becomes possible to reduce the total size of the inventory or of the funds committed. Indeed, techniques and equipment have been developed and already implemented which permit the obligation of funds by a digital computer as the need arises or which permit posting inventory changes as they occur and the consequent initiation of replenishment action at the most favorable time for doing so.

It is well to note that the *theories* which would provide for the optimum utilization of capital or of inventory stocks have been known to economists for some time. It is only within the past few years, however, that the *means* have been available—in the form of the digital computer system —to effect these theories in actual practice. The almost universal availability of these powerful clerical tools now makes it technologically possible for American business to employ the theories; their widespread application, however, must await the solution of a great many related sociological problems.

Automation in Banking. Entire books have been devoted to the very interesting and rapidly developing subject of automation in banking. In the present volume, our purpose is only to outline briefly the progress which has already been made, the development presently under way, and our guess as to what the automated banking system of the future will look like.

In 1958, the 15,000 banks comprising the private banking system in this country processed checks at the rate of about 10 billion annually. It was anticipated by banking officials that this rate would increase to about 14 billion checks annually in 1960 and to about 20 billion checks annually 10 years thereafter.

These figures are so large that their significance is difficult to comprehend. However, as a result of the very large volume of transactions presently handled, to which volume must be added an extremely rapid growth, it seems easy to predict that electronic data processing techniques *must* be employed widely by the future banking industry. It seems clear to data processing specialists and bankers alike that mass data-handling techniques must be developed and utilized if our banking service is to maintain its present level of efficiency.

Probably the most widely publicized avenue employed to attack the bank data processing problem has been that of machine reading of printed characters. Machines have been developed which are capable of reading material printed in magnetic ink. This ink is endowed with special magnetic properties so that a magnetically sensitive mechanism can detect its presence or absence. The information thus detected by the machine is interpreted as a set of codes, each of which is automatically translated into its alphabetical or numerical equivalent. The result of this translation is then recorded by the machine in a form—such as punched tape, punched cards, or magnetic tape—which can be read conveniently by some other element of the digital computer system in which it operates.

Very similar devices have been developed which read ordinary printed matter photoelectrically, i.e., by detecting light or darkness in designated areas of the paper. Once these devices have detected the information printed on the page, they may operate in exactly the same manner as described above.

There is a great deal of information to be read from each check written in today's American banking structure. It has been estimated that before a check is returned to the maker the dollar amount is read an average of thirteen times, nationally. Other information on the check, designating the maker, the payee, the bank, and the date, must be read accurately several times for each check, although not so often as the amount itself. Whenever any information must be read and manually entered on some other document more than once, the possibility that automatic information-reading techniques may increase efficiency suggests itself.

The present approach to this problem involves the use of automatic character-reading devices. The static information (bank, account number) read by these devices can be preprinted on the check so that it need not be manually read by the banking system even once. Variable information, designating the amount and the payee, is reentered onto the check (at the point where the check enters the banking system) in machine-readable form by a manually operated key-driven device. Thereafter it can be read in the same fashion as the preprinted information.

These techniques, in test at several places in the United States but not in widespread operational use, promise a significant increase in the efficiency of the banking operations of today. Probably of more importance is the fact that they seem to offer a hope to that industry for handling the banking loads of tomorrow.

The future need for a modernized check-reading system as well as its technological feasibility has been well established. As before, the problem becomes one of people—mainly bank customers—and this time, by virtue of its very large scope, truly a sociological one. Resistance to conformity, based on both logical and illogical grounds, is the cornerstone of the difficulty. People—both makers and payees of checks—must fit their checking habits into the pattern created by machines whose flexibility is greatly limited as compared with the vast numbers of clerks they are intended to replace.

Although we seem to be limited to persuading these people to conform on a voluntary basis to the requirements of any new checking system, some past efforts in this direction have had results so poor that the small increase in conformity noted could be explained away by random fluctuations of check-writing habits. Other such efforts, perhaps notably connected with plans to introduce a large-scale digital computer system into the record-keeping operations of the bank itself, have met with a negligible amount of customer *resistance*. The inability to predict accurately the customer attitudes which will be encountered and consequently the measures necessary to circumvent them is likely to delay substantially the modernization of large-scale check-reading systems. Coming only with experience, this customer confidence is seen to be the essential to the success of automatic systems.

An interesting alternative to any attack on the check-reading problem is one which involves the direct transfer of funds from the bank to the individual or organization in whose favor they should be drawn without the intermediate use of a check of any kind. Additionally, such a concept might involve the use of a credit card of some sort on the part of both the payer and the payee. By such a device, it might be possible to enter automatically all the information except the dollar amount involved into the system.

Similar systems are under development or in use at the

present time, although they are somewhat less automatic than that described. Some commercial banks now offer a plan whereby charge purchases can be made at any member sales outlet and billed in a single bill monthly by the bank. The addition of automatic sales data entry and the automatic transfer of funds from the buyer's account to that of the sales outlet will provide us with a highly efficient operational method for monthly charge payments.

Computers in Air Traffic Control. Commercial and other civilian aircraft as well as most military aircraft flying over the continental United States are at the present time controlled by the Federal Aviation Agency (FAA) by means of twenty-nine air route traffic control centers (ARTCC) located at key air-route points throughout the country. People called "air-traffic controllers" in each such center are generally responsible for the job of keeping track of all airplane flights in such a way as to avoid conflicts of any kind between them.

These controllers are responsible for the preparation of paper strips with information giving aircraft identification, route, altitude, and estimated arrival times written on them. These strips are prepared on the basis of information received from air carrier companies, military air agencies, and adjacent ARTCCs. A single center may be required to prepare many thousand such slips daily. From the information on these slips, estimates of flight arrivals over FAA check points must be calculated. This key calculation permits the rapid identification of conflicting flight plans which, when noted, are changed appropriately by the cognizant controller.

Several years of careful planning have recently culminated in the insertion of a digital computer system into the problem at one such center to handle the very large volume of clerical work involved. The computer promises to automate completely all this routine information handling and calculation, thereby freeing the air-traffic controller to carry out his basic responsibilities of flight monitoring and control. It is planned that all twenty-nine centers will be so automated by 1962.

The apparent success of this operation is very likely due at least in part to the fact that the computer has not been required to deal with the general public but has instead been inserted into an environment which was already very carefully controlled. There are relatively few commercial and military agencies upon which each computer will depend, and each is subject to the very close control of the FAA in this matter. In addition, very significant efforts have been made to organize the computer operation so that it will be able to deal with the same types of information as are used in the manual system which it will replace.

Here, then, is an almost ideal application for computers: The environment is carefully controlled; the computer portion of the problem is very well defined; the data-handling requirement is relatively high and moreover is growing very rapidly; the requirement for accuracy, speed, and thoroughness is high; and finally, the application, once in successful operation at one of the many centers, can be implemented almost without alteration at each of the others.

It is rare to find a data processing application where the weak points of the present system are precisely the strong points of a digital computer system to be installed. It seems fortuitous that an operation whose failures have been highlighted by widespread publicity as well as tragedy is amenable to so nearly a complete revision and improvement in so short a time.

Centralized Data Processing. The goal of centralizing all data processing activities of a single organization in a single place has long been the dream of advanced thinkers in the field. The meaning of "centralizing," however, varies greatly with the organization involved. This meaning ranges from centralization to a single point in a retail store, through a single point in the city, a single point in the state, and finally to a single point in the nation.

Many stores have centralized the processing of their data for all departments at a single point in the store. Several city governments have centralized at least their financial operations at a single point in the city. A large oil company has centralized its state-wide activities at a single point, even including the mathematical calculations necessary for optimal refining processes. And an electronics firm, an appliance firm, an auto firm, an airline organization, several railroads, and many others have already centralized their data processing activities successfully on a national scale.

This rush to centralize was first generated on the basis of the direct cost savings in data processing. The fact that this did not prove to be realistic in most cases was highly publicized in the beginning. Then, however, when the opportunity to take a second look at centralized data processing was forced on us, we observed that, while the costs of doing the job were often no less than those in a decentralized system (and were sometimes more), the increased capability to control the operations of the organization in an integrated fashion represented a far greater advantage.

It developed that, by centralizing the data processing involved, we had the means to reduce inventories, balance sales, direct advertising campaigns at critical areas, and minimize inequities in management. Some large manufacturing organizations have been urging the Federal Communications Commission to grant permission for them to install private microwave data links between each of their manufacturing plants and a single data processing center at the corporate headquarters. By so doing, the headquarters could be in a position to control the operations of each manufacturing plant on an almost instantaneous basis for the purpose of maximizing the achievement of the objectives of the firm as a whole.

In spite of the sociological difficulties with which this high degree of automation would be fraught—as described in several previous chapters—these firms now feel confident that its successful achievement will provide them with benefits which warrant the risks involved. While the immediate feasibility of these benefits is perhaps open to some question, their eminently practical future now seems beyond any reasonable doubt.

Automation in Reservation Systems. Among the most highly perishable commodities for sale today in the American market are the airline reservation, the railroad reservation, and the hotel reservation. Accommodations in airplanes, trains, or hotels are limited in number and so are in some danger of being "oversold." At the same time, those which are not sold are valueless to the vendor as soon as the airline flight departs, the train leaves, or the hotel room lies empty overnight. It is further true that the customers for these commodities are drawn from the public at large; therefore, it is of prime importance to maintain good relations with that general public, in terms of reservations reliably and promptly made.

A successful solution to these problems involves the aggregation at a single point of information received at widespread geographical points corresponding to those at which reservations are sought by potential customers. The digital computer, with a recognized capacity for aggregating information, and augmented by specialized equipment for entering information into the system at distant points and transmitting it to the computer, seems ideal for the solution. On a somewhat limited scale this has already proved to be true. Present plans make it possible to predict that by 1965 no major airline or passenger railroad will be without a reservation system based on a digital computer. It is probable that every large national hotel chain will install such a system even sooner.

The use of a computer in a reservations application differs from most of the other uses we have described. In the first place, the computer so utilized is usually devoted entirely to the problem of reservations, rather than being asked to deal now with inventory, now with financial accounting, and now with payroll. This is necessary in order that, in a relatively simple system, the computer can be available rapidly to handle requests for reservations made at any time of the day or night against the inventory of unused spaces maintained in its external "storage."

The second distinctive characteristic of this application of a digital computer is that the input to the computer is entered by (and the outputs are destined for) sales agents untrained in computer system techniques. The entire computer operation is organized to facilitate the determination by agents of the operating firm as to whether spaces are available to be reserved and upon such affirmative determination to enter the reservation and reduce the inventory of available spaces accordingly.

In order to make it possible for these agents, trained in the ways of sales, reservations, and dealing with the public but not in the ways of computers, successfully to enter information into the system, special devices have been developed which check the information entered for completeness, accuracy, and relevancy. These devices are located on the agent's desk at the point where he normally carries out his reservation business. They are connected by teletype or telephone lines directly to the computer system itself. Buttons on the device are operated by the agent to acquire the information desired, and replies from the computer are registered by the same device in terms of lights or punches in cards.

In the airline field especially, the extremely rapid increase in business and consequent expansion of the systems has prompted the statement from many authorities to the effect that the handling of reservations will soon be a data processing task so large that it will be physically impossible to handle it without the aid of a computer. Such systems, linking several hundred agents' sets in three or four cities, are already in operation. Additional plans are now being implemented by a few large airlines to link almost a thousand such sets to a single reservation computer, with links among as many as 120 communities in the United States, Canada, Bermuda, and Puerto Rico subsequently slated. The final steps in airlines reservation development is likely to be the linking of the automatic reservation systems of all the major airlines serving the United States into a single gigantic network for automatic reservation making. The high incidence of cross ticketing and the major size of the airline funds tied up in this operation seems sure to dictate the eventual amalgamation of the ticketing operation.

Very similar in operating characteristics to the airline system, the hotel reservation system will enable large hotel chains to react as a unit to requests for reservations, with any member hotel acting as a reservation agent for any other. The initiation of a reservation at any hotel in the chain will cause a reservation slip to be prepared automatically at the desired hotel for filing there until the reservation can be utilized. The hotel problem, large as it is, is somewhat less dynamic than the airline one and is therefore likely to be in operation much sooner in some hotel chains. A semiautomated approximation to the system described is already in use by several of these chains.

The Service Bureau Business. The rapid expansion of the market for digital computer applications has generated several organizations devoted to the cause of carrying out data processing operations on behalf of commercial customers who do not care to devote their own equipment to this job. Thus, if one organization has a payroll operation requiring about an hour of computer time per week, it is advantageous for that organization to have its computing done by a service bureau and pay only for the time used.

These service bureaus may be operated either privately for the profit-making purposes of the owner of the service bureau—as well as, presumably, for the benefit of the firm for which the service is done—or as cooperative organizations for the mutual benefit—as well as any possible mutual detriment—of all the members. Both forms are rather common, although the first category is dominated by the activities of the manufacturers of computing equipment themselves. A modified form of the service bureau concept is exemplified by the use by one firm of a computer leased or owned by another organization on the basis of a pay-as-you-use arrangement with that organization. The services provided by these several forms of "bureaus" are truly varied. Some will simply provide the computer on which to run the problem. Others will additionally provide the personnel to run the machine. Still others will add services to help in preparing the problem for machine solution, or even help to analyze the problem itself for a preferred system of computer solution. But the ultimate in service offered is the service bureau which will come into the customer's business operations (for these are never cooperative service bureaus), completely describe the problems to be solved by computer techniques, outline the method of their solution, create the detailed machine procedures, and carry out these procedures on the bureau's own machines as often as required.

The service bureau concept, in one form or another, promises to provide the means for extending the application of digital computers into vast areas otherwise capable of resisting the advance for many years.

Computers in Government. With its requirement to carry out activities in the field of data processing increasing at a rate unique in the field, the Federal government has turned to digital computer systems for help on an ever-broadening scale. The massive problems of the Census Bureau were the first to receive assistance in this fashion. The Department of Defense and its predecessors have been in the computer business for almost 20 years, starting with ballistics calculations at the beginning of World War II. Now other departments such as the Social Security Administration, the Treasury Department, and the Department of Agriculture have become active in the computer field, along with other agencies directly concerned with our national defense.

The National Bureau of Standards of the Department of Commerce has entered not only the field of computer applications but the field of computer engineering. On some occasions, that bureau has underwritten hardware development by private industry, while in other cases it has undertaken to accomplish the development work itself. Its most noteworthy work has been the actual construction of two operating computers, one in Washington, D.C., and one in Los Angeles, the development of film-reading devices for census and other agencies, and the development of equipment pertaining to the long-sought "automatic post office" for that department.

It seems likely that the early activities of the Federal government in the computer field provided to private industry both the incentive and the financial support necessary for the present advanced level of computer hardware development. Thus we have experienced a period during which the Federal government has been able not only to further its own interests by participating in research and development activities but to provide at the same time financial support essential to the continued growth of a major new industry.

State, county, and local governments have also been interested in the developing computer field. Some examples of recent applications of computers to the data processing problems of these governments will illustrate their growing interest in the field.

The state of Pennsylvania has begun operations on a computer at the state capital to carry out most of the clerical operations of a financial nature for the entire state. The state of California is planning a digital computer system to maintain all the records for its Department of Motor Vehicles and to prepare registration slips for motorists. And, in a joint effort with the U.S. Bureau of Public Roads, Cook County, and the city of Chicago, a computer-oriented project of the state of Illinois is carrying out the analysis necessary for the long-term planning of metropolitan Chicago's public and private transportation facilities.

Several county governments have turned to digital computers in order to accomplish their massive clerical jobs within set budget limitations. Probably the largest such application is that in Los Angeles County, where the initial application will compute the tax bills for well over a million taxpayers in the area concerned.

New York City is using the entire daytime capacity of a large-scale computer solely for preparing the payroll and carrying out related operations for its more than 200,000 employees. New Haven, Connecticut, is managing all its financial appropriations from a single point with a modest computer installation, thereby permitting the responsible city agency to exercise the financial control with which it is charged. Engineering calculations required in the departments of public works and other departments are common applications of digital computers within the structure of city government.

These state, county, and city applications are very broad of scope. Additional computer applications include financial accounting, income tax calculation and payment recording, real property tax computations, gasoline tax collection and refunding, motor vehicle registration, welfare management, highway cost accounting, payroll preparation, and highway and storm-drain engineering calculations. Yet at this point the surface has hardly been scratched. It has been estimated that the use of computers can reduce the number of full-time employees required for these data processing functions by almost 50 per cent and that the seasonal employees previously required can be virtually eliminated. The new-found ability to accomplish the data processing required in government and at the same time to hold firm or possibly reduce the costs incurred thereby has aroused the interest if not the complete confidence of even the most conservative of public officials. As these benefits are demonstrated on an increasing scale and scope, the remaining conservatism in organizational and political attitudes now hindering the advance of data processing will fade before the devastating onslaught of modern equipment and techniques.

New vistas for computers

The history of human endeavor reveals that our very objectives are defeated whenever, in the interests of conservatism and the consolidation of acknowledged gains, we fail to reach out continually for greater and still greater gains in any field of endeavor. Thus, in the field of digital computers, research money must be spent by potential manufacturers, risks of deviating from proved systems into newer and presumably much better ones must be taken by equipment users, and a general attitude of trust and willingness to experiment—in search of great advantage—must be assumed by the public at large.

We have already described applications of digital computers to a rather wide range of existing problems which had formerly been solved in less efficient ways. It seems appropriate now to mention some applications of digital computer equipment and techniques, both present and projected, to problems whose solution had not previously been systematized or automated in any fashion.

Automatic Reading of Handwritten Symbols. In several laboratories throughout the country, devices capable of "reading" handwritten symbols and translating them into machine-readable form have been successfully demonstrated. Most of these devices provide for the transcription of symbols, stylized only very loosely, with a special pencil into a prescribed area of the object form. The presence of a pencil mark is then detected at several points within the area by one of several techniques. The code thus formed is a digital code which is translated by the machine into punches on card or tape or into magnetic tape recording.

The purpose of such a device is to eliminate the need both for manual *re*transcription of information which has already been manually transcribed and for specially trained operators for devices which will record directly in machine language. For example, long-distance telephone operators in the Bell system are presently required to create about 2 billion long-distance tickets annually, each with from twenty to thirty handwritten characters. In this situation, the advantages of cost and timeliness are vividly evident. They result from not requiring the telephone operator to manipulate special devices for creating computer input information and at the same time eliminating the need for the manual retranscription of this information.

The computer processing of this information, which will occur subsequently—including customer billing, traffic analysis, and system planning by statistical criteria—will increase substantially the efficiency of the telephone system. The economics of carrying out these same activities without the aid of digital computer techniques would be prohibitive.

Computers and Music. The application of digital computers to the field of music probably borders on the frivolous (although there are those who contend that there are serious purposes to be served thereby), but it is nevertheless interesting to consider.

By providing it with an audio output system, a computer can be applied directly to the problem of sound production. The frequency of the sound produced constitutes a series of musical notes. It is similarly possible to cause a computer to control devices which are designed to depress valves or keys of ordinary musical instruments or to draw a bow across a string upon which mechanical "fingers" have been appropriately placed. In this fashion an entire orchestra can be operated under computer control so that it will play any musical selection written. Finally, it is possible to cause a computer to develop, according to mathematical criteria and the "rules" of note sequences and harmony, the harmony or the orchestration for a given sequence of musical notes, or even to develop an *original* sequence of notes and hence to write music.

The rendition of familiar airs in a single-note fashion has actually become rather common in computer circles today, especially around Christmastime. Usually producing an oboelike sound, the output of the computer is easily identified as to the musical number it is rendering. In a similar manner, computers have been programmed to generate the sounds which constitute one part in a trio, the other two parts of which are rendered by human musicians or in some cases by the computer itself.

Little if any effort has been devoted to the problem of causing a computer to operate an otherwise standard musical instrument such as a trumpet or a violin. This is due, we suppose, to the lack of a device for the computer to control which in turn is capable of operating the musical instrument in question. The development of such a device is clearly feasible, but the benefits associated with such a development do not obviously warrant the expense. It is interesting to speculate, in this same vein, as to why no computer has yet been programmed to operate a piano by actuating mechanisms much the same as those employed in the standard player piano.

Finally, some work has indeed been done by computers in the area of musical composition. But efforts to date have been limited to attempts to produce simple melodies in the fashion of humans. The computed music results from the generation of numbers corresponding to the frequency of musical notes by the computer. Actually the computer is potentially much more powerful than that. It is capable of "writing" and "playing" pieces which are timed to the millionth of a second; one or a group of computers are capable of rendering an almost unlimited number of parts; and all other musical facets, such as tempo changes and tonal shades, can be controlled to a heretofore unknown degree of preciseness. Although the number of musical combinations achievable is not infinite, a computer can achieve a very large number of different effects so that no undue repetitions can be detected.

Probably, in the final analysis, it is this very preciseness which limits the computer's effectiveness in this area. Lacking qualitative judgment and "feeling" will forever be the undoing of the digital computer in the field of music.

Identification of Criminals. The identification of criminals by identifying their fingerprints and their personal appearance (in coded form) can now be accomplished automatically by digital computer techniques. The usefulness of these techniques in terms of speed and accuracy is such as to mean the quick apprehension of criminals who otherwise would escape the hands of the law.

To accomplish this job, a basic file of the characteristics of individuals must be compiled. In order to do this, previously obtained finger prints are classified according to the number of "loops" which appear in the print of each finger. If all ten fingers are recorded, such a classification can identify 10^{15} (1 million billion) different individuals. In addition to fingerprints, the file also contains in coded form such individual characteristics as height, weight, scars, marks, teeth, and clothing, as well as *modus operandi* of known criminals, such as weapon used, usual object of crime, usual time of crime, and noticeable personal habits.

When a crime is committed, as much of the above information as possible is obtained about it. Suitably coded, it is compared automatically with the information already recorded in this master file and the file entries corresponding to suitable suspects are retrieved from the file.

In addition to the advantages of speed and accuracy mentioned, several other perhaps equally important advantages can be attributed to automatic searching of the files. The first of these is that any combination and even all the characteristics known can be sought simultaneously. Secondly, allowance can be made for human error, either in the original preparation of the file or the identification or coding of the evidence received, by causing the machine to search for a *range* of values within those particular characteristics categories which allow for ranges. And finally, the difficult to acquire skilled personnel—who have been occupied with the routine task of criminal identification file searching—can be freed for the qualitative aspects of file search where their experience-bred judgment is really required.

Industrial Planning by Digital Computer. With the aid of a digital computer, the Swedish State Power Board has been able to determine the most effective use of Swedish hydroelectric power, the country's main source of industrial power. Involving the comparison of a great many possible plans in terms of established criteria, the job would have required many months and involved great expense if carried out manually.

The problem was to determine the efficiency of a particular plan for the distribution of the available electric power as a function of the relative economic importance of the five industries considered. The first step was to prepare a set of mathematical equations which would, for each plan, define the relationship among such factors as winter ice, steam-power production, water level in reservoirs, capacity of dams and turbines, and the export of electricity to Denmark. Solutions to this set of equations according to the established criteria were then computed for each plan and the results compared.

Another kind of industrial planning is that which involves the so-called "management game" and often involves a digital computer as an agent of the judge. One such game directs a competition among fictitious supermarket chains established in a mythical city. These chains compete by making decisions relative to the sale or purchase of units, the remodeling of old units, the operating cash position they wish to maintain, the market research in which they want to engage, the advertising they want to purchase, and the gross margin objective as a per cent of sales.

These decisions, made at hourly intervals designed to represent quarterly operating periods of real grocery chains, are entered into the computer as the variables of the equations which have already been coded into the computer storage. Although each of the teams operates during the "quarter" without any knowledge of what the other teams are doing, the computer equations are so written as to take into account the effect of the decisions of one chain (e.g., a decision to double the advertising budget) on the profits of another (e.g., which at the same time has decided to discontinue advertising altogether).

The value of games of this type lies in the fact that, when they are played by executives actually involved in a similar business as a part of their daily life, these men are able to note the effect of several rather gross types of decisions and trends in the game situation, and thereby to take account of these effects in real life. Since the value of the game obviously increases with its realism and faithfulness to real life, the factors of familiarity with the business gamed, cleverness in simulation, and effectively reflecting the business complexity in the computer equations combine to make the management game a tool of increasing usefulness in the industrial scene.

Digital Process Control. Of particular interest in the field of controlling the events which take place in industrial processes (such as automobile production lines or crude-oil refining) is the promise of the digital computer to provide a logical basis for their control at the same rate at which the processes must take place. Such a computer can automatically "read" instruments which reflect the status of the process, enter the corresponding values into equations in its storage, perform calculations which determine the particular actions that will result in nearly optimum process operation, and activate or deactivate the appropriate process mechanisms.

This computer can translate incoming data into an appropriate form, perform a wide range of mathematical and logical computing operations, start up or shut down devices, compare instrument readings with previously defined standard conditions, select material flow paths, and check its own operations. Some such processes which are performed or contemplated today are actually so complex as to preclude the exercise of any real control over them by manual means. Other processes, while feasible to control manually, cannot be so controlled at a cost which will make the product marketable. For these reasons, the coming widespread use of digital computers in the field of industrial process control promises to make the marketplace for the resulting products a much more interesting and accessible place.

The Broadening Scope of Mathematical Applications. The recent advent of the digital computer has made it practical to extend the application of relatively complex mathematical techniques into fields in which they were previously unknown. These methods have made it possible to introduce systematic, rational, and completely unemotional problem-solving techniques into areas where they seemed to have been completely lacking. The scope of application has been very wide and we mention only a few of them here for illustrative purposes.

One area of business in which decisions have seemingly been based on judgment, intuition, and background of knowledge gained only from experience has been that of stock-market investments. Although these aspects of human decisions have not been entirely eliminated, a digital computer has now been applied to a major portion of the problem. By means of the mathematical techniques of "linear programming," a digital computer has been programmed to compare all the possible investment opportunities of which it is informed according to criteria previously established. On the basis of these criteria—which include the objective of the investment program as well as facts about the stocks such as price, past earnings, dividend record, and the estimated future performance—the computer can then produce its recommendation as to the most suitable portfolio for the purpose indicated. Because of its very high speed and capacity for storing facts, this computer is able to select the "best" portfolio from among a group of possibilities which is very large indeed.

Medical research is another field which is beginning to get some rather important direct benefits from the digital computer. Equipment and techniques now under development will, when perfected, assist medical diagnosis by correlating data on disease occurrences and computing their probabilities accordingly. It is further expected that, by these methods, the analysis and correlation of symptoms by computer techniques will permit the detection of trends in a particular case much earlier than presently. Such a system might perform its analysis on data entered directly from the patient himself by means of devices which would read instruments attached to the patient so as to reflect his condition. Another possibility, of course, would be to record the desired data in a more or less usual manual fashion and then retranscribe it into machine language and enter it into the machine system. Probably the main advantage of any of these systems is that diagnosis of the available information is by well-defined systematic means and is far more likely to be accurate and sufficiently broad of computational scope than diagnosis by present techniques.

By means of the capability to compute provided by digital computers, the techniques of mathematical probability and statistics have been employed on an ever-widening scale to problems of our everyday lives. One such application, for example, deals with the problem of purchasing an automobile for private use. According to the alternatives given for a particular case which was presented to the computer—the costs of the car specified, the operating expenses and their rate of increase, the decreasing probability that the present car would last another 3 months, and the trade-in deals available—analysis revealed that the most favorable deal from the buyer's point of view, financially, is to buy an automobile 3 years old and trade it in on another 3-year-old car when the first one is 6½ years old.

Another problem of similar structure deals with a question of interest to baseball players and fans alike: For each situation which may be encountered, what strategy of base-stealing, bunting, and "swinging away" should be employed? The computer solution to the problem was alarmingly simple: Always swing away. The analysis carried out by the computer of the statistics involved indicated that, no matter the skills of the particular players involved as regards base stealing or hitting, it is "better" to try for a hit than to resort to any bunting or stealing strategy. Having defined "best" to cover games won over an entire season rather than any individual game, the computer analysis found further that each game should be played for itself without regard to considerations such as fatigue and even strategy which seemed to pertain to future games.

The Dead Sea Scrolls. A major contribution to an increased knowledge of our cultural background has been the translation, with the aid of a digital computer, of the now famous scrolls found only recently in the Biblical areas of the Middle East. The scrolls, over twenty centuries old, were broken and otherwise deteriorated. They were written over a rather long period of time, over the span of which new words came into the language and old ones changed their meaning. Since accurate translations can be produced only in a precise context for every word, it became necessary to relate individual words on the scrolls not to modern-language transliterations but to the context in which they were written.

Thus the alphabetical word index of the scrolls which was produced and translated into computer language had to be studied in each context in which every word appeared. Not only were many words missing, but entire sections of the writings had crumbled to dust. Thousands of words found on floors of caves had to be fitted into their proper place in the proper scroll. By reference to the individual word index in the machine storage, every possible use for each such fragment was determined, and on the basis of the statistics generated, a qualified guess as to the word originally written was made wherever these words were mutilated beyond recognition. Possible words which might fit into the gap created by the mutilated word were examined by the computer until the one was found which fitted best into the context provided by the readable words on each side of this gap. Such extensive perusal of the dictionary created would have involved a lifetime of work for experienced scholars if the computer had not been available to perform the job in a few hours.

The technique of replacing words by noting their context was tested for accuracy and the results are interesting. By inserting a text of known composition and an appropriate index, the computer, by use of these techniques, was able to insert as many as *five consecutive* missing words into their proper context.[1] It seems clear that, although we cannot guarantee a substitution of the missing words which duplicates exactly the original ones, the statistical techniques employed and the vast amount of data which can be considered can provide a far more acceptable solution by digital computer means than by the manual efforts of any reasonable number of experts.

Ad Infinitum. We could continue to mention applications of digital computer techniques to problems everywhere in our society almost without limit. Further, there are surely

---

[1] An extension of the same technique into the field of analyzing the style of any author by studying the frequency, use, and sequence of the words he employs suggests itself.

a great many such applications which have never come to our attention. Therefore, we shall limit ourselves to the mention of only a few more, each rather briefly, in the hope that the reader will be motivated to discover still more applications in the literature or in fact.

A small digital computer has been employed as an aid in the rescue of persons from ships at sea. The method employed is to store in the computer storage information regarding ships at sea in a given area. Ships will report their destination, course, speed, and position to the computer at regular intervals after they leave port. Whenever such a ship signals that it is in trouble, or whenever such a periodic report is not received, the machine can then update its position as well as that of all other ships in the area, so as to determine which ship should be requested to go to the aid of the ship in distress.

By a mathematical manipulation of the output of a device which translates human speech into a numeric code, a digital computer has simulated the transmission characteristics of long-distance transmission systems which are under study. By eliminating the need actually to construct each system which must be studied, the use of a computer has resulted in major dollar savings in research in these systems as well as the extension of the scope of this research to new and otherwise untapped techniques.

By a somewhat similar technique, a computer has been able to "identify" and "reproduce" pictorial information. A photograph mounted on a rotating drum is scanned photoelectrically in a few seconds. The output of the scan, in terms of its position around and along the drum, is coded by letting 1 signify dark and 0 signify light. By interpreting this code, a computer has been able to determine the number of distinct objects in the picture, to recognize particular chemical and electrical diagrams for what they represent, and automatically to produce contour maps from photographic information on which the appropriate analysis has been performed.

Because it has not been practical to employ voting machines widely throughout the country, several devices have been developed, each for the purpose of counting and tabulating the votes recorded manually on ordinary paper ballots. The most successful of these computers can count up to twenty complete ballots per second with as many as fifty votes per ballot, automatically feed the ballots and stack them after they are counted, take account of format changes which occur over the situations represented in a given election, and act as a referee when any improper voting procedures—such as more than one vote for a single office—occur. It has been estimated that manual counting of ballots can result in about one error for every two ballots counted. Some experts will not guarantee the results of any large manually counted election within a margin of 4 per cent of the total vote. The increased accuracy provided by these computers, along with the sharp reduction in precinct workers which they permit, may have a drastic effect on our voting procedures and their frequency in future years.

Machine abstracting and the translation of languages

One field of development in which the digital computer will play a major role promises to alter substantially the character of organizations, of countries, and of the world itself. This field is that of communications among men.

Carried out by either the written or the spoken word, the free flow of information among men is limited both by language barriers and by barriers imposed by the sheer volume of information to be communicated. Recent developments have indicated that digital computer techniques will be instrumental in bridging both these barriers to a very substantial degree and that the major impact of this development can be expected to take place within the current century.

Abstracting by Digital Computer. The feasibility of creating abstracts of technical papers has already been demonstrated by several groups working in the field. Although several techniques have been employed, probably the most promising one is that of statistical abstracting. The method of statistical abstracting involves an analysis by a computer of the frequency with which particular words and combinations of words appear in the text to be abstracted. A table is then created on the basis of this analysis and the computer then analyzes each sentence in the text and assigns a significance factor, based on this table, to it.

The computer is then in a position to select the highest-ranking sentence or sentences and print them out. This information constitutes the abstract desired and can be made as cryptic or as comprehensive as required by imposing limits in terms of length and computed rank to its contents.

While the usefulness of such automatically created abtracts seems apparent, several technical problems remain. It is necessary, for example, for the original article which is to be subjected to the automatic abstraction process first to be recorded in machine language so that the information contained therein can be entered into the machine for analysis. The magnitude of performing this job by manual means for a library of, say, 1 million volumes, is staggering. It represents perhaps in the neighborhood of 30,000 man-years of effort. The solution to this problem is not far from at hand. Machine techniques for automatically reading printed characters have already been proved on a very limited scale, and their improvement to a level of operational usefulness seems only a matter of time.

The problem of utilizing the group of abstracts which have been created appears at first glance to be an equally perplexing problem. Here, too, recent developments of hardware promise a satisfactory solution. If the abstracts created for the 1 million volume library mentioned above average 200 alphabetic characters in length, devices are now under development in our computer laboratories which will be capable of reading the entire automated library of abstracts and selecting only the desired entries in only 10 seconds. As the development of these devices progresses, they will acquire the ability to select and present to the human seeker of knowledge all the abstracts in the library whose contents deal with the subject about which information is sought.

The uses for the automatic accessibility of published information are legion. It has been estimated that in excess of 50 per cent of the research carried out today is duplication of efforts previously put forth. The amount of duplication which occurs is increasing at a rapid rate. Perhaps, in combination with new techniques for translation of languages like those described below, this program of automatic abstracting will make available knowledge of a major portion of the research already accomplished. Only then will it be possible to heed the advice of Thomas Edison to "stand on the shoulders of others."

Machine Translation of Languages. Until very recently, efforts in the United States to develop a theory and a method of practical application for the translation from a "source" language to an "object" language by digital computer techniques could be described as negligible. Several significant efforts in this direction are now under way, partly as a result of a recognition of the basic fact that digital computer systems are capable of accomplishing this vital task. But it is likely that the primary reason for this recent spurt of activity is the discovery that many such efforts, involving major resources and world-famous mathematicians and scientists, are presently under way within the scientific community of the Soviet Union.

Initially directed in the United States at the problem of gaining a better understanding of Russian scientific and philosophic thought, and therefore initially concerned primarily with translation from Russian to English, the efficient translation from one language to another has a much broader purpose to achieve. The National Science Foundation has said that all basic scientific research is profoundly dependent upon the fullest possible dissemination of information now published in thirty to thirty-five different languages and that the most effective aid in this dissemination would be prompt translation of the published material into a language which the interested reader can understand.

The problem of machine translation can be divided into four parts: input, storage, computation, and output. The input problem is to convert printed information into machine language and is peculiar in that it deals with a large volume of information that is physically difficult to handle. The storage problem is primarily that of storing a glossary of the relevant languages in the machine system so that its availability to the machine is adequate; although the total storage thus involved may be very large indeed, the nucleus of words which are subject to frequent use and so are needed rapidly may indeed be manageably small. The computational problem is to look up words in the glossary, to analyze the sentence structure of the text to be translated, and to recognize and resolve by logical means the multiple meanings encountered. The output problem is to convert the coded representations of object-language words produced by the machine into ordinary matter printed in the object language, where here the problem may be peculiar not only because of the large volume but because of the very large number of different symbols which must be printed.

Largely because of devoted individual efforts, the development of a theoretical basis for machine translation is fairly well advanced in this country. In the areas of empirical research and analysis, where large commitments of dollars and personal efforts are required, the development of machine translation is lagging. Efforts are required to prepare texts to be translated, to analyze and classify the words in these texts into useful glossaries, and to prepare and refine continuously computer programs which are capable of making full use of the results of this textual analysis.

But in all these areas we find large recent increases in the programs which are under way. It seems that in a very few years we shall see suitable automatic equipment to read printed matter, large "random access" storage devices with a ready accessibility of the information contained therein, glossaries based on extensive analyses of Russian texts, and highly sophisticated computer programs capable of making complex logical decisions to produce accurate readable English text.

In the longer run, we can look forward to the automatic almost immediate translation of significant written pronouncements from the original source language to every important object language which remains. As the computer industry moves closer to this objective, so the world moves closer to mutual understanding and cooperation.

Index

Abacus, 26
Abstracting written material, 237–239
Access, random, 53–58, 154, 206
    sequential, 53–55
Access time, 102
Accuracy, 80–81
Advertising, 162–163
Air traffic control, 85, 212–214
Airline reservations, 41, 49, 215–218
Automatic reading of information, 133–134, 223–224
Automation, attitude of labor force toward, 183–187
    misconceptions on, 194–195
Automobile purchase investment, 232

Babbage, Charles, 27
Baldwin Calculator, 27
Banking, computers in, 208–212
Baseball, computer analysis, 232
Batch processing, 53–54
Berkeley, Edmund C., 108
Burroughs Listing Accountant, 27
Business objectives, 45, 63, 190

Capital, utilization of, 207–208
Centralized data processing, 214–215
Character reading, 209–210, 223–224
Check-reading devices, 209–211
Checkers, 99, 107, 109
Chess, 99, 102, 105–107, 109
City governments, computers used by, 222
Climate for growth, 199–202
Communications, 40–41, 59–62
Complex information processing, 103, 108
Complex interactions, 12, 84, 175
Complex operations, 12–14, 103–110, 174
    key developments in, 108–109
Computer, central processing unit, 28–30
    control, 28, 54–55
    cost, 16–17, 42, 56–57, 61, 74–77
    design (see Design)
    difficulties, 80–89
    history, 18–20, 23, 26–28
    impact, 202
    installation, management problems, 1–3, 176–182

Computer, logical operations, 48,
  102
  misconceptions on, 3–4, 180–
    182, 194–196
  objectives, 10–12
  power, future requirements for,
    122–124
  psychological role, 178
  reliability, 126–127
  response, 58–59
  size, 42–43
    future, 121–122
  speed, 49
    future, 124–125
  standardization, 153
  storage (*see* Storage)
Conformity in business activities,
  193
Control, 28, 54–55
Credit card application, 204–205,
  211
Criminal identification, 226–228
Customer credit, 47
Customer service, 206–207

Data, accumulation of, 66–68
  for decision making, 110–114
  operational, 68–70
  presentation of results, 71–74
Data processing, 4–10
  centralized, 214–215
  cost of, 16–17
  definition of, 4–5
  elements of, 65–66, 70
  increasing volume of, 14–16
  phases of, 5–6
Data processing specialist, 78
Dataphone, 61, 62
Dead Sea Scrolls, 233–234
Decision making, complex opera-
    tions in, 103–110
  in computer installation, 177

Decision making, data for, 110–114
  definition of, 94–96
  elements of, 96–103, 111
  human elements, 114–119
  psychological barriers, 178–180
Design, circuit, 141
  component, 140–141
  equipment, 141–143
  in future, 138–145
  large-scale EDP system, 44–62
  system, 142
  total, 143–145
Digital control, 40, 229–230

Economic factors, 199–202
Electrical communications, simula-
    tion, 235
Engineers in research, 156–157
Equipment, design techniques,
    141–143
  fitting to jobs, 45–48
  future developments, 127–138
  general considerations, 48–59
  maintenance, 169–172
  operation, 167–169
Errors, 81–82, 112, 191–192
  corrections as cause of, 59
  human, 12–13, 81, 191
  transistorized devices, 126
External storage, 31, 131
  permanently accessible, 129–131
  size, 50–51
  types, 51–54

Failure of computers, 83–84, 87,
  126
Feasibility studies, 164
Federal Aviation Agency, 212, 213
Federal Communications Commis-
    sion, 215

Files, conversion of, 67–68
  large, 53
  revision needed in, 66–68
Fingerprints, identification of, 226–227
Flexibility of operation, 83
Future developments, 17, 20–22, 120–148
  growth of computer systems, 201
  power, 122–124
  reliability, 126–127
  size, 121–122
  speed, 124–125
  storage capacity, 125–126
  system described, 145–147

Governmental applications of computers, 199, 220–223

High-speed printer, 135–136
History of computers, 18–20, 23, 26–28
Hollerith, Dr. Herman, 27
Hotel reservations, 215, 216, 218

Increased capital utilization, 207–208
Indexing, 55
Industrial planning, 228
Industrial process control, 229
Information, accumulation, 66–68
  organization, 138–140
  presentation, 71–84
  retrieval, 139
Information processing, 28, 70, 111
  complex, 103, 108
Information storage (*see* Storage)
Input, 33–36, 66, 138
  errors, 191
Inventory management, 13, 46, 50–51

Job displacement, 184

Kineplex, 61, 62

Labor-management relations, 182–189
Labor unions, attitude toward automation, 184–187
Large files (*see* Files)
Large-scale EDP system, design, 44–62
  in future, 145–147
  installation, 63–65
  operation, 66–93
Life insurance application, 179
Logical operations, 48, 102

Machine translation, 239–241
Magnetic card, 131, 134–135
Magnetic disk, 53, 130
Magnetic tape, 33, 38, 53, 56, 127–129, 131
Maintenance of equipment, 169–172
Management, labor relations, 182–189
  policies, 1–2, 78–79
  problems in introduction of computers, 176–182
Management games, 228–229
Manufacturer, 149–172
  objectives, 150–154
  research and development, 155–162
  sales and applications, 162–167
Marconi box, 27
Marine rescue, 235
Mathematical applications, 230–233
Media, input, 36
  output, 38
  storage, 31, 131

Medical research and diagnosis, 231
Miniaturization, 121
Music, applications to, 224–226
  audio output of computers, 225

Napier, John, 26
National Bureau of Standards, 158, 220
Nerve cells, 143

Odner, W. T., 27
On-line processing, 53–54, **87, 88**
Order repertoire, 132–133
Organized labor (see Labor unions)
Output, 36–40, 71

Parmalee Calculator, 27
Pascal, Blaise, 26
Pattern recognition, 108
Pay television application, 205–206
Payroll, 50
Pictorial reproduction, 235–236
Planning, by computers, 228–229
  long- and short-range, 89–93
Programming, 24, 105
Punched cards, 36, 38, 152
  history of, 27–28

Racetrack, calculation of odds, 188–189
Random access, 53–58, 154, 206
Reliability of equipment, 126–127
Rescue at sea, 235

Research, 149, 155–162
Reservation applications, 215–218
Retail sales application, 202–204

Sales of computers, 163–165
Sequential access, 53–55
Service bureaus, 218–220
Shipping, decisions in, 52
Social Security Administration, **68**
Speech, recognition, 137
  translation into code, 235
Stock-market investments, 231
Storage, 29–32, 102, 105
  external, 31, 50–54, 129–131
  future developments, 125–126, 129–132
  internal, 30, 49, 130
Storage media, 31–33, 131
Storage unit, 31–32
Stored program computers, 24–25
Strategy, 45–48, 58
System, EDP (see Large-scale EDP system)
System design (see Design)

Tax application of computers, 202
Television, pay, 205–206
Transceiver, 61
Translation, of languages, 239–241
  of speech into code, 235

Universal programming, 25
Users' organizations, 168

Vote-counting machines, 236

Warehousing application, 206